# Multicultural Art Activities

### From the Cultures of Africa, Asia and North America

## Grades 2–5

Written by Darlene Ritter
Illustrated by Diane Valko
Edited by Judy Urban

**CTP** ©1993, Creative Teaching Press, Inc., Cypress, CA 90630

## Introduction

The art projects in *Multicultural Art Activities* give students opportunities for creative expression and help develop an appreciation for the cultural heritage of the peoples of Africa, Asia, and North America.

*Multicultural Art Activities* contains art projects from three continents—Africa, Asia, and North America. The 44 projects selected represent countries and regions studied in a majority of 2nd through 5th grade classrooms. In many cases, these geographic areas also reflect the cultural heritage of large student populations. Based upon authentic arts and crafts, the projects in *Multicultural Art Activities* are made from easily available materials and adapted for use in the 2nd through 5th grade classrooms.

*Multicultural Art Activities* includes projects that reflect both ancient and modern cultures. Ancient cultures produced some of the most beautiful art and exciting artifacts ever made. Art and craft techniques have been passed from generation to generation ensuring their survival. They are an expression of the cultural past and heritage of people all over our planet. Through art, we can learn about the history and customs of other peoples. These projects can become a link with the long ago or far away as well as with our neighbors today.

Since many cultures have similar crafts, it is often possible to adapt a project from one country or region to another. Tie-dye fabric, for example, is as appropriate for a study of Africa as it is for India. Shields were used in Africa as well as in North America. Masks are a part of African, Chinese, Japanese, Mexican, and Native American cultures. Similarly, fans, hats, and kites cross cultural and geographic boundaries. As you study a culture, look for ways of adapting the projects presented. Often this can be done by following the basic construction techniques and varying only colors and motifs.

## How to Use Multicultural Art Activities

Look through the book and select a project or technique representative of the culture you are studying. A summary and map precede each section. Historical background is provided for each project. A list of materials, suggestions for teacher preparation or notes to the teacher, and illustrated directions follow. For maximum flexibility and originality, one or more variations are listed for each project, and ideas are offered for integrating the art projects into other areas of the curriculum. Literature selections precede each section listing children's books available for multicultural studies. Optional reproducible patterns for some projects are located in the back of the book.

The projects in *Multicultural Art Activities* can be successfully completed by students at many different grade levels. Teachers can make adjustments for the age and developmental level of individual students and for the number of students in the classroom. The basic construction of the project can be completed by most students. Older students will be able to complete the projects with greater attention to detail and decoration. They will also be able to finish more of the variations suggested and add creative elements to the projects.

Be sure to show students the photographs and sketches of the project in this book and pictures of related art and artifacts from other books before beginning the actual project. When possible, complete the project yourself before using the lesson with students. The teacher is the best judge of the needs of individual students or classes.

# Table of Contents

# Literature Selections for Africa

Aardema, Verna. *Bimwili and the Zimwi*. Dial, 1985.

_____. *Bringing the Rain to Kapiti Plain*. Dial, 1981.

_____. *Why Mosquitoes Buzz in People's Ears*. Dial, 1975.

Bang, Molly. *Ten, Nine, Eight*. Greenwillow, 1983.

Bryan, Ashley. *Beat the Story-Drum, Pum-Pum*. Atheneum, 1987.

Carue, Jan. *Children of the Sun*. Little, Brown, 1980.

Daly, Niki. *Not So Fast, Songololo*. Atheneum, 1986.

Dayrell, Elphinstone. *Why the Sun and the Moon Live in the Sky*. Houghton Mifflin, 1968.

Dragonwagon, Crescent. *Half a Moon and One Whole Star*. Macmillan, 1986.

Feelings, Muriel. *Jambo Means Hello: Swahili Alphabet Book*. Dial, 1976.

_____. *Moja Means One: Swahili Counting Book*. Dial, 1972.

French, Fiona. *Aio, the Rainmaker*. Oxford University Press, 1975.

Fulton, Eleanor, and Pat Smith. *Let's Slice the Ice: A Collection of Black Children's Ring Games and Chants*. Magnamusic-Baton, 1978.

Greaves, Nick. *When Hippo Was Hairy and Other Tales From Africa*. Barron, 1988.

Greenfield, Eloise. *Africa Dream*. HarperCollins/Crowell, 1989.

_____. *Night on Neighborhood Street*. Dial, 1991.

Grifalconi, Ann. *Darkness and the Butterfly*. Little, Brown, 1987.

_____. *Osa's Pride*. Little, Brown, 1990.

_____. *The Village of Round and Square Houses*. Little, Brown, 1986.

Haskins, Jim. *Count Your Way Through Africa*. Carolrhoda, 1989.

Howard, Elizabeth F. *Aunt Flossie's Hats and Crab Cakes Later*. Clarion, 1991.

Isadora, Rachel. *At the Crossroads*. Greenwillow, 1991.

Kerwen, Rosalind. *Legends of the Animal World*. Cambridge University Press, 1986.

Kimmel, Eric. *Anansi and the Moss-Covered Rock*. Holiday House, 1990.

Knutson, Barbara. *Why the Crab Has No Head: An African Folktale*. Carolrhoda, 1987.

Lester, Julius. *How Many Spots Does a Leopard Have and Other Tales*. Scholastic, 1989.

Lewin, Hugh. *Jafta*. Carolrhoda, 1983.

Lottridge, Celia B. *The Name of the Tree: A Bantu Folktale*. Macmillan, 1990.

Margolies, Barbara A. *Rehema's Journey: A Visit in Tanzania*. Scholastic, 1990.

Mattox, Cheryl W. *Shake It to the One That You Love the Best: Play Songs and Lullabies From Black Musical Traditions*. Warren-Mattox, 1990.

McDermott, Gerald. *Anansi the Spider: A Tale From the Ashanti*. Holt, 1972.

McKenna, Nancy Durrell. *A Zebra Family*. Lerner, 1986.

Mollel, Tololwa M. *The Orphan Boy*. Ticknor and Fields, 1991.

Musgrove, Margaret. *Ashanti to Zulu*. Dial, 1976.

Naidoo, Beverley. *Journey to Jo'burg*. HarperCollins, 1986.

_____. *Chain of Fire*. HarperCollins, 1990.

San Souci, Robert. *Sukey and the Mermaid*. Four Winds Press, 1992.

Seeger, Pete. *Abiyoyo*. Macmillan, 1986.

Serfozo, Mary. *Rain Talk*. McElderry Books, 1990.

Steptoe, John. *Mufaro's Beautiful Daughters: An African Tale*. Lothrop, 1987.

Stuart, Gene S. *Safari*. National Geographic Society, 1982.

Tadjo, Véronique. *Lord of the Dance: An African Retelling*. HarperCollins/Lippincott, 1989.

Ward, Leila. *I Am Eyes, Ni Macho*. Greenwillow, 1978.

Williams, Karen Lynn. *When Africa Was Home*. Orchard/Watts, 1991.

_____. *Galimoto*. Morrow, 1991.

# African Art

Sahara
Desert

Nile River

Niger River

**Benin** *

**Ghana** *

Lake Victoria

* Mt. Kilimanjaro

Kalahari
Desert

**A**lthough modern Africa has great cities and thriving commercial centers, tribal life and culture continue to define the continent. In Africa tradition is very strong, and age-old arts and crafts continue to flourish. The arts and crafts of Africa are expressions of tribal life and the vehicle by which Africans transmit their cultural heritage from one generation to another. Sculpture, pottery, basketry, and personal decoration tell us about the peoples who created them, their systems of value and belief, and their ways of life. Most African art is functional and plays a part in everyday life. This is particularly true of the visual arts of painting and sculpture. With its bold patterns, bright colors, simplified or exaggerated forms, and superior craftsmanship, African art makes a direct and irresistible appeal to the senses.

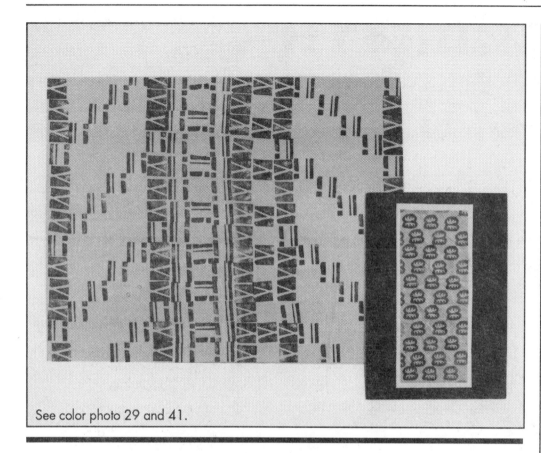

See color photo 29 and 41.

## Materials

- brown paper sacks or wrapping paper 9" x 12" or larger (one per student)
- Styrofoam™ packing blocks as used for packing large appliances (cut in 2" squares)
- black tempera paint
- brushes
- large paper clips
- pencils
- fine-line markers
- tape
- scissors

# Adinkra Designs

Adinkra cloth, made by the Ashanti people of Ghana, conveys the thoughts and feelings of the wearer by means of traditional symbols. The fabric is divided into squares by lines drawn with a bark dye and stamped with designs carved from gourds. Adinkra symbols express such qualities as patience, strength, security, defiance, and forgiveness. Originally worn at funerals to bid good-bye to the departed, adinkra cloth is worn on many special occasions. Once black or red-brown with glossy black designs, adinkra fabrics now include bright colors ■

## Adinkra Designs and Their Meanings

1. **Royalty**: the most important design
2. **Forgiveness**: turn the other cheek
3. **Fern**: defiance
4. **Moon and star**: faithfulness
5. **The king's eye**: the king sees all
6. **Heart**: patience and endurance
7. **Sanctity**: good fortune
8. **Star, child of the heavens**: I depend on God alone
9. **Ram's horns**: strength
10. **Link or chain**: human relationships

## Procedure

**1.** Look at the photograph on page 6 for ideas. Cut the paper bags or wrapping paper into pieces of the desired size (9"x12" or larger). Use fine-line black markers to divide the brown paper into large sections. Draw "stitches" with markers around the edges of each section to give the appearance of fabric.

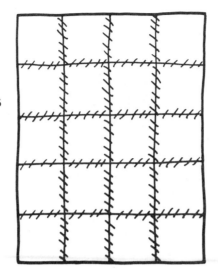

**2.** Keeping in mind that the design will print in reverse, draw a simple stamp design on a piece of Styrofoam block with a pencil. Refer to the adinkra symbols for ideas. Press the pencil into the Styrofoam as you draw. (Paper clips can be used instead of pencils as tools to make a deep groove.)

## Variations

■ Substitute ink stamp pads for tempera paints.

■ Use fabrics such as muslin or old sheets.

■ Use potatoes or gum erasers for stamps.

## Integration

■ Make adinkra book covers for African reports.

■ Dress dolls in African costumes of adinkra cloth.

■ Write about a person. Choose adinkra designs that symbolize that person and illustrate.

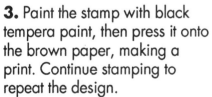

**3.** Paint the stamp with black tempera paint, then press it onto the brown paper, making a print. Continue stamping to repeat the design.

**4.** When dry, tape students' designs together to make a class adinkra paper fabric.

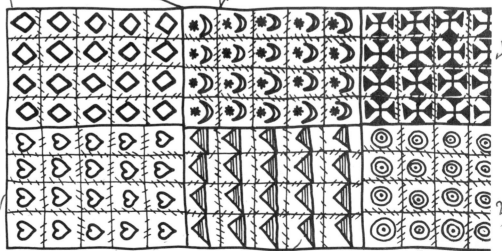

See color photo 38.

# Skin Decoration

## Materials

- white drawing paper, 9" x 12" (one per student)
- pencils
- markers

**S**kin decoration is common among men and women throughout the world. In Africa there are many forms of skin decoration. Some are permanent, like tattoos and scarification (cutting the skin to make scars), while others are temporary, like body or face painting. Among the Yoruba, skin decoration indicates family affiliation. Among the Nuba, it marks the stages in a woman's life. Many tribes paint the face and body for aesthetic effect or in preparation for tribal rituals. For special rituals, some Africans paint their bodies to look like animals, hoping in this way to assume the animal's power ∎

## Procedure

**1.** Look at the photograph of the project on page 8 and other pictures of skin decorations. Place your hand (fingers open) and forearm down on the paper and trace around it with a pencil. Go over this line with a marker.

**2.** Use your imagination and draw decorative designs on the arm and hand. Draw your designs with black or brown markers, then fill them in with colored markers. Design rings and bracelets, too.

## Variations

■ Try decorating with animal markings like leopard spots or tiger stripes.

■ Make a self-portrait and decorate it.

■ Work in groups to decorate a full body outlined on paper.

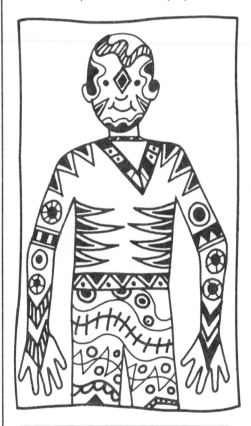

## Integration

■ Write 10 adjectives describing the person who would wear your hand design. (Example: *bold, brave, young.*) Write a poem or story about this make-believe character.

■ Relate skin decorations to clowns and their unique makeup.

See color photo 5.

# Woven Container

## Materials

- paper cups or bowls used for warp spokes, 5 oz. or 6 oz. size (one per student)
- yarn, raffia, or twine used for weaving
- scissors
- glue

## Teacher Preparation

For younger children, cut bowls or cups into $\frac{1}{2}$" or $\frac{3}{4}$" wide spokes of *uneven* number. Cut as close to the bottom as possible. Older children can cut an *even* number of spokes and follow the directions for pairing weaving. They can use more colors and a variety of yarns to produce patterns in their weaving.

**A**frican baskets come in all shapes and sizes. They are made from a variety of natural materials—raffia, reeds, grasses—or materials obtained from trade, and most are decorated with stylized geometric designs. Some baskets are used only in religious ceremonies, while others have practical uses. African women make the baskets needed for home use. Basketry using "pairing weaving" is typical of the Gold Coast, now known as Ghana. In pairing weaving, the warp (hard foundation strands called spokes) consists of an even number of spokes. Two weft (soft strands used to weave over and under the warp and sometimes called weavers) are used. ∎

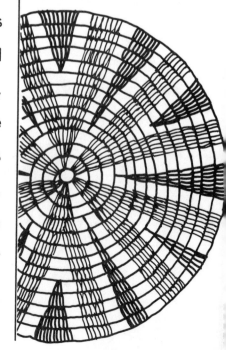

# Procedure

**1.** Cut the cup or bowl into spokes (foundation, warp) that are about ½" wide. (Pairing weaving requires an *even* number of spokes. Standard weaving requires an *uneven* number.)

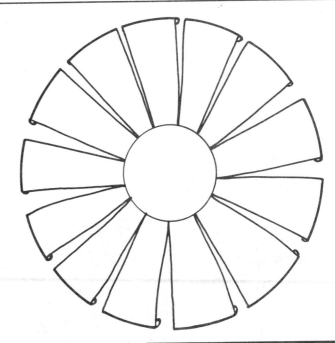

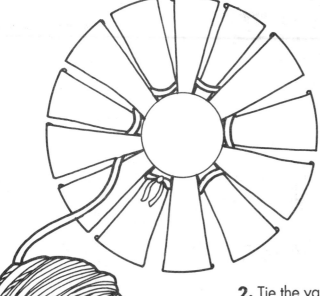

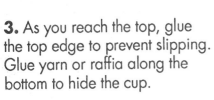

**2.** Tie the yarn around a spoke and start to weave. In pairing weaving, go over two spokes and under two spokes. To change colors, tie the ends of the yarn together.

**3.** As you reach the top, glue the top edge to prevent slipping. Glue yarn or raffia along the bottom to hide the cup.

# Variation

■ Use a paper plate or tagboard instead of a bowl and make a hot pad from the weaving.

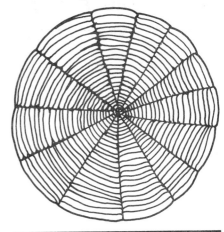

# Integration

■ Have an African market and barter for the containers or their contents. Students can practice walking to market with baskets full of various materials balanced on their heads.

See color photo 20.

- black construction paper, 9" x 12" (one per student)
- scraps of colorful construction paper
- scissors
- glue
- black markers, black crayons, or black ink pens

# Paper Appliqué

Dahomey appliqués were originally a royal art form. Craftsmen at the palace of the king at Abomey [symbol] sewed colorful symbols to a black background, creating fabrics for banners, flags, tents, and [symbol] wall hangings. These appliqués told the history of the Kingdom of [symbol] Dahomey by displaying the attributes of successive kings. Today Dahomey is the West African nation of Benin, [symbol] the palace at Abomey is a museum, and talented craftsmen make cloths, not for the monarch but for tourists ▮

## Procedure

**1.** Using assorted colors of paper scraps, design and cut out symbolic shapes representing Africa.

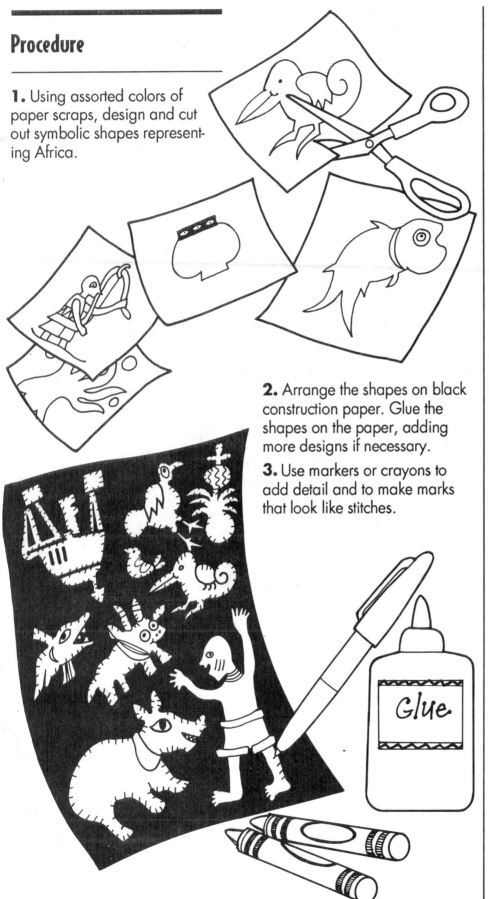

**2.** Arrange the shapes on black construction paper. Glue the shapes on the paper, adding more designs if necessary.

**3.** Use markers or crayons to add detail and to make marks that look like stitches.

## Variations

■ Sew shapes of material onto fabric instead of paper.

■ Put all of the appliquéd pieces together to make one large wall mural.

## Integration

■ Tell autobiographies with appliqués.

■ Make a pictorial history of your school or town into a banner. Donate the banner to your school's office.

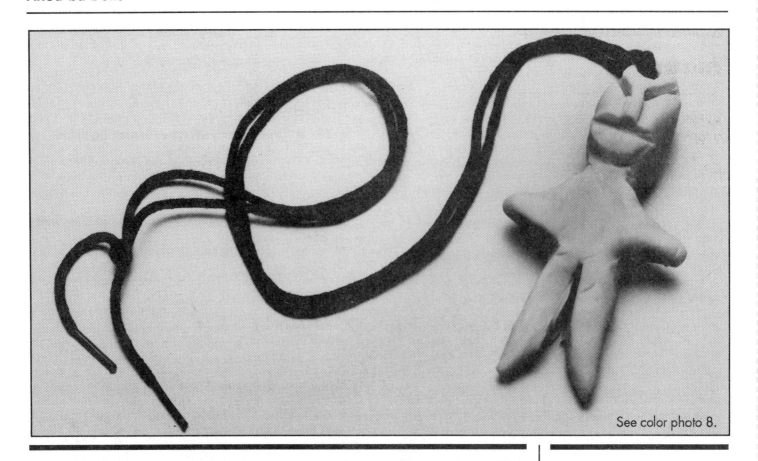

See color photo 8.

# Akua-ba Dolls

In Ghana, Ashanti women wore small figures called *akua-ba* dolls around their necks or carried them in their pockets. They believed that these dolls would help them conceive and would ensure the birth of a healthy and beautiful child. The dolls had three basic head shapes: an oval head was thought to bring a girl baby, a square head a boy baby, and a round head a wise baby

## Materials

- modeling clay or dough which can be baked or fired (2" ball per student)
- craft sticks or toothpicks
- wax paper
- yarn or string
- rolling pins or large dowel sticks for rolling clay

## Teacher Preparation

Show students examples of akua-ba dolls from this book and other resources.

# Procedure

**1.** Flatten clay to ⅓" thick. Use a toothpick or craft stick to form the body and to add the details.

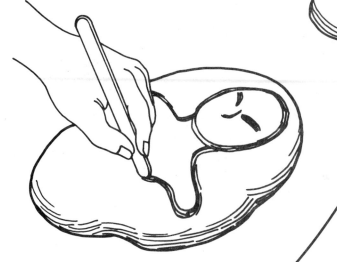

**2.** If the doll is to be worn as a necklace, make a hole in the top. Dry the clay on wax paper, and bake or fire according to the manufacturer's directions.

**3.** Thread the hole with yarn or string long enough to go over the wearer's head.

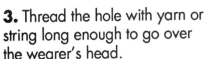

# Variations

■ Carve a doll out of a bar of soap.

■ Dress dolls in homemade African costumes.

■ Stain and varnish dolls to create an antique look.

■ Make dolls from tagboard.

# Integration

■ Little Ashanti girls played with akua-ba dolls. Find out about dolls that children have played with throughout history.

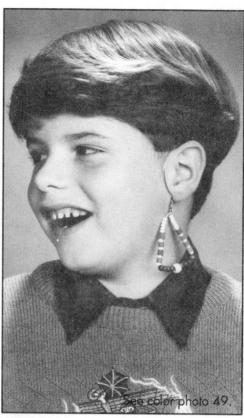

See color photo 49.

# Jewelry From Beads

Throughout Africa men and women wear jewelry to enhance their appearance  and to indicate their social status or wealth. In addition to bracelets, earrings, necklaces, and anklets, some Africans wear nose ornaments, lip jewelry, waist rings, and hair or hat pins. Some jewelry is believed to have magical powers. Many Africans wear amulets, or good luck charms, to protect them from danger or illness. The most valuable jewelry is cast from precious metals. Beaded jewelry is especially popular in southern Africa, where beads are made from many different materials, including glass, wood, clay, stones, and shells ▪

## Materials

- dry salad macaroni (3 lbs. per average class of 30)
- food coloring
- rubbing alcohol
- small resealable sandwich bags
- string, yarn, or elastic thread
- clear tape
- variety of odds and ends that can be used for beads (sequins, buttons, shells, broken necklaces, or clay beads)
- picture wire and metal curtain rings 1½" diameter

## Teacher Preparation

Depending on the age of your students, you can color the macaroni beads ahead of time as described below, or students can color the beads and trade them. Use the beads for any of the jewelry projects. *Note: The food coloring will come off if the jewelry gets wet.*

## Procedure

Color macaroni for beads. Put 1/2 tsp. of alcohol in the corner of a resealable plastic bag. Add a few drops of food coloring. (The more drops, the more intense the color.) Add a handful of macaroni. Seal the bag and shake until all the macaroni is dry. (The alcohol dries the macaroni.) If it is still damp, spread it out to dry.

## Boy's Earrings

**1.** Twist the picture wire to form a triangle with one long end. String small beads on the wire, placing a large bead in the middle of the lower side.

**2.** Fasten wire together at the top, and make a loop to fit over the ear.

## Necklaces and Bracelets

Cut strings long enough to fit over the head or hand easily and allow for tying. Knot one end of the string several times, and wrap the other end with tape to make it easier to thread through the bead. String the macaroni. Students may want to use patterns; for example, a repeating pattern of 3 reds, 2 blues, 1 white. Other odds and ends can be strung along with the macaroni.

## Girl's Headdress

**1.** String a single strand of picture wire to make a row of beads that will fit across the top of the head, and string another strand to go around the forehead. Twist the wires to join the two.

**2.** Attach a curtain ring to the intersections on both sides of the headpiece. String three rings of beads and attach them to the curtain ring to create ear coverings.

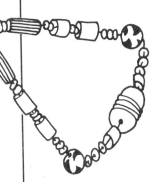

## Variations

■ Make hair pieces, earrings, rings, or ankle bracelets.
■ Make cutouts of large torsos and dress them with the beads.

## Integration

■ Wear jewelry with African clothing for a performance of African dance or music.
■ Write a story, identifying the main characters by the type of jewelry they wear.

See color photo 14.

# Masks

## Materials

- neutral colored (brown, white, tan, black) construction paper, 12" x 18" (one per student)
- scraps of construction paper
- scissors
- glue
- yarn, twine, raffia, buttons, beads, leather or fabric scraps, shells, seeds

**T**here are three basic kinds of African masks: the helmet mask, which covers the wearer's entire head; the face mask, which covers only the face; and the headdress mask, which sits on top of the head. Masks served religious or magical purposes. They were worn during tribal rites that maintained social order, commemorated the dead, celebrated victories in battle, and prepared the young for adulthood. Made by specially trained artists, most masks were carved from wood and engraved or painted with geometric designs. Sometimes long grass or raffia was attached to the bottom of the mask. Teeth, hair, shells, beads, metals, or stones were added ∎

# Procedure

**1.** Draw a large outline of a face on construction paper to make the mask's base. Cut it out.

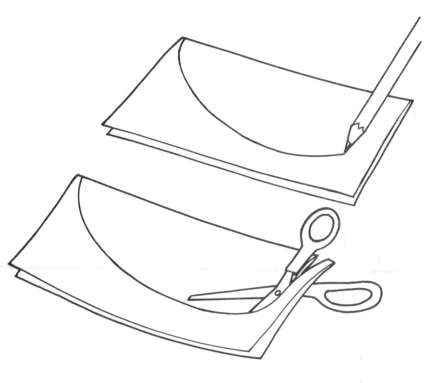

**2.** Glue large geometric shapes to the front of the mask and layer smaller shapes to them. Exaggerate the facial features. Cut out eye slits.

## Variations

■ Use a paper plate for the mask base. Decorate with paint.

■ Use plaster cloth from a craft store, and follow directions for using it directly on a child's face. Build up, exaggerate, and distort the features. Allow mask to dry, then decorate.

**3.** Cut 1" slits at the four corners of the mask, overlap them and staple or glue to give the mask shape.

**4.** Add odds and ends to decorate the mask.

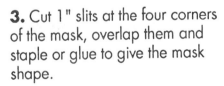

## Integration

■ Write stories about ceremonies where masks are worn. Dramatize a ceremony, with students holding masks before their faces.

## Cambodia

Lee, Jeanne M. *Silent Lotus.* Farrar, 1991.

Roland, Donna. *Grandfather's Stories From Cambodia.* Open My World, 1984.

Wall, Lina M. and Cathy Spagnoli. *Judge Rabbit and the Tree Spirit: A Folktale From Cambodia.* Childrens Press, 1991.

## China

DeJong, Meindert. *The House of Sixty Fathers.* HarperCollins, 1987.

Demi. *The Empty Pot.* Henry Holt, 1990.

Grafton, Carol Belanger. *Authentic Chinese Cut-Paper Designs.* Dover Books, 1988.

Hillman, Elizabeth. *Min-yo and the Moon Dragon.* Harcourt, 1992.

Hume, Lotta Carswell. *Favorite Children's Stories From China and Tibet.* C. E. Tuttle, 1962.

Kendall, Carol. *The Wedding of the Rat Family.* Macmillan, 1988.

Morris, Winifred. *The Future of Yen-Tzu.* Atheneum, 1992.

Lattimore, Deborah Nourse. *The Dragon's Robe.* HarperCollins, 1990.

Levinson, Riki. *Our Home Is the Sea.* Dutton, 1988.

Lobel, Arnold. *Ming Lo Moves the Mountain.* Greenwillow, 1982.

Neville, Emily Cheney. *The China Year.* HarperCollins, 1991.

Pattison, Darcy. *The River Dragon.* Lothrop, Lee, 1987.

San Souci, Robert. *The Enchanted Tapestry.* Dial Books, 1987.

Schlein, Miriam. *The Year of the Panda.* HarperCollins/Crowell, 1990.

Thompson, Peggy. *City Kids in China.* HarperCollins, 1991.

Vá, Leong. *A Letter to the King.* HarperCollins, 1991.

Yen, Clara. *Why Rat Comes First: The Story of the Chinese Zodiac.* Childrens Press, 1991.

Yep, Laurence. *The Rainbow People.* HarperCollins, 1989.

_____. *Tongues of Jade.* HarperCollins, 1991.

Yolen, Jane. *The Emperor and the Kite.* Putnam, 1988.

Young, Ed. *Lon Po Po.* Putnam, 1989.

## India

Bond, Ruskin. *Cherry Tree.* Caroline House, 1991.

Bonnici, Peter. *The Festival.* Carolrhoda, 1985.

Towle, Faith M. *The Magic Cooking Pot: A Folktale of India.* Houghton, 1975.

Kamal, Aleph. *The Bird Who Was an Elephant.* HarperCollins/Lippincott, 1990.

Kipling, Rudyard. *Just So Stories.* HarperCollins, 1991.

Rodanas, Kristina. *The Story of Wali Dâd.* Lothrop, 1988.

Siberell, Anne. *A Journey to Paradise.* Holt, 1990.

Wettasinghe, Sybil. *The Umbrella Thief.* Kane/Miller, 1987.

## Japan

Baker, Keith. *The Magic Fan.* Harcourt Brace, 1989.

Bang, Molly. *The Paper Crane.* Greenwillow, 1985.

Buck, Pearl S. *The Big Wave.* HarperCollins/Crowell, 1973.

Coerr, Eleanor. *Sadako and the Thousand Paper Cranes.* Putnam, 1977.

Hwang, Joyce. *Kirigami One.* Heian International, 1991.

Johnston, Tony. *The Badger and the Magic Fan.* Putnam, 1990.

McDermott, Gerald. *The Stonecutter.* Puffin, 1978.

Suetake, Kunihiro. *Red Dragonfly on My Shoulder.* HarperCollins, 1992.

Jacobsen, Karen. *Japan.* Childrens Press, 1982.

Johnson, Ryerson. *Kenji and the Magic Geese.* Simon and Schuster, 1992.

Laurin, Anne. *Perfect Crane.* HarperCollins, 1981.

Okawa, Essei. *The Fisherman and the Grateful Turtle.* Heian International, 1985.

Pittman, Helena Clare. *The Gift of the Willows.* Carolrhoda, 1988.

## Korea

Ginsberg, Mirra. *Chinese Mirror.* Global Village, 1988.

Haskins, Jim, and D. Hockerman. *Count Your Way Through Korea.* Carolrhoda, 1989.

Jacobsen, Karen. *Korea.* Childrens Press, 1989.

Kim, Edward. *Facts About Korea.* Heian International, 1986.

Paek, Min. *Aekyung's Dream.* Childrens Press, 1988.

## Laos

Jacobsen, Karen. *Laos.* Childrens Press, 1991.

Xiong, Blia, and Cathy Spagnoli. *Nine-in-One, Grr! Grr!.* Childrens Press, 1989.

## Philippines

Aruego, Jose. *Rockabye, Crocodile.* Greenwillow, 1988.

Roland, Donna, and Ron Oden. *Grandfather's Stories From the Philippines.* Open My World, 1985.

## Thailand

Caraway, Caren. *Southeast Asian Textile Designs.* Stemmer House, 1983.

Jacobsen, Karen. *Thailand.* Childrens Press, 1989.

Thompson, Ruth and Neil. *A Family in Thailand.* Lerner, 1989.

Orihara, Kei and David K. Wright, ed. *Children of the World: Thailand.* Gareth Stevens, 1988.

## Vietnam

Surat, Michele. *Angel Child, Dragon Child.* Scholastic, 1989.

Lee, Jeanne M. *Toad Is the Uncle of Heaven.* Holt, 1985.

Nhuong, Huynh Quang. *The Land I Lost: Adventures of a Boy in Vietnam.* HarperCollins, 1990.

Jacobsen, Karen. *Vietnam.* Childrens Press, 1992.

Roland, Donna. *Grandfather's Stories From Vietnam.* Open My World, 1984.

# Asian Art

**T**he fine, folk, and decorative arts

of Asia emanate from ancient cultures. Thousands of years, ago, for example,

Chinese civilization was highly developed when life in the West was relatively primitive.

**T**raditional arts and crafts are practiced throughout Asia today. In India, China, Japan,

and Southeast Asia, artisans turn out a dazzling variety of craftwork, from fans to dolls, kites, and

paper cuts. A highly developed aesthetic sense is evident in everything Asians make, from simple

straw hats to porcelain vases. The arts of Asia, whether they are produced in the

bazaars of India or the villages of Thailand, reflect the unique qualities of the continent's peoples,

their ways of life, and religious beliefs.

See color photo 37.

# Paper Appliqué

Laos, a Southeast Asian nation of four million people, was once called the "Land of a Million Elephants." In the past, elephants were treated like royalty and adorned with jewels. Today, elephants play an important role in many Laotian festivals and are treated with great respect. Equally important to the economy of the country, elephants are used as work animals ▪

## Materials

- elephant pattern on page 98
- white or gray construction paper, 3" x 18" (one per student)
- dark construction paper, 4" x 18" (one per student)
- scissors
- glue
- fine-line markers
- sequins
- wallpaper, wrapping paper, or fabric scraps

## Teacher Preparation

Prepare the elephant pattern for each student to trace.

## Procedure

**1.** Fold the white or gray construction paper in half (3" x 9") and fold in half again (3" x 4½").

**2.** Trace the elephant pattern on the folded construction paper, making sure the trunk and the tail touch the folded edges.

**3.** Cut out the elephant. (Be careful not to cut the elephants apart at the trunk and tail.) Unfold the paper carefully to reveal four connected elephants.

**4.** Glue the four elephants on the dark construction paper background, and use markers, sequins, scraps, and your imagination to decorate the elephants with different patterns. A blanket, or a hat can be added if desired.

## Variation

■ Fold a piece of black paper in half and cut out an elephant shape leaving the top of the elephant uncut along the fold. Open the cutout and glue the symmetrical elephant design on a paper of contrasting color.

## Integration

■ Find more information about elephants and report on them to the class.

■ Make elephants out of clay and create an elephant caravan with the clay figures. Write an adventure story about it.

See color photo 35.

## Materials

- water
- large mixing bowl
- measuring cup
- plaster of paris (casting plaster)
- large mixing spoons
- clean, empty milk cartons or plastic containers (one per student)
- carving tools (table knives, paper clips, nails, pennies, nail files, craft sticks)
- sketch paper
- pencils
- sandpaper or emery boards
- carbon paper

# Plaster Bas-relief

**A** bas-relief is a shallow sculpture which projects from the surface of a wall. Many extraordinary relief carvings are found in Angkor, the one-time capital of the Khmer Empire, now a ruined city in the depths of the Cambodian jungle. The reliefs of the city's great temple complex, Angkor Wat, date from the 12th century when Khmer kings ruled large areas of Southeast Asia. Some of the finest reliefs represent *apsaras*, the celestial beauties of Hindu mythology with their elaborate clothing, jewelry, and towering crowns ∎

## Notes to the Teacher

The first variation may be easier to use with younger children since they are familiar with plasticine clay. Also, this technique eliminates the drawing and transferring of the design to the plaster as well as the need to carve. The only difference is that the relief forms in reverse on the plaster. (Objects molded in relief in clay will be indented in the plaster.)

## Procedure

**1.** Mix two parts plaster of paris and one part water in a large bowl. Let the mixture set for two minutes. Stir just until smooth; over-stirring will cause air bubbles. Pour enough plaster into each container to make a layer ½" to ¾" thick and let harden. When the plaster is dry it will be hot.

**2.** While the plaster is drying (preferably several hours), draw sketches of godlike dancers on paper, perhaps one with several arms or heads. Keep the sketches simple, and be sure they are the size of the plaster block in the container.

**3.** Tear the paper or plastic container away from the plaster. Transfer the sketch onto the plaster using carbon paper.

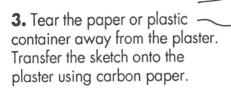

**4.** Use tools to carve away the background, leaving the dancer design standing out in relief. When completely dry, refine and smooth the carving with sandpaper or emery boards.

## Variations

■ Cast a relief instead of carving one. Use a ¾" layer of plasticine clay in the bottom of the container and mold a relief on this layer. Using a paintbrush, coat the plasticine clay well with liquid dish soap and allow to dry. Prepare plaster according to the directions in step 1 and pour over the clay to a depth of about ¾". Dry at least two hours, then carefully remove the container and the clay. (Remember, this casting method will form the relief in reverse. Things molded in relief will be indented in the plaster.) Refine and smooth the plaster relief you have cast with sandpaper or emery boards.

■ Imagine that you are an artist hired to design a bas-relief for your school or some other public building. Make models of your bas-relief designs in clay.

■ Make stands for the finished bas-reliefs, and display the reliefs or arrange them in a line to resemble a temple wall.

## Integration

■ Write a story to go along with your bas-relief. Create a dance to dramatize the story.

See color photos 28 and 42.

# Textural Rubbings

## Materials

**T**he making of rubbings is  a favorite pastime of many travelers, art lovers, and history buffs. Travelers to faraway Cambodia often make rubbings of the relief carvings at the world-famous temples of Angkor. Some make their impressions with a special moistened paper which hardens in the form of the bas-relief when it dries ■

- large sheets of newsprint (one per student)
- dark crayons with the paper removed
- construction paper, 6" x 9", for frames (one per student)
- sandpaper, cheese graters, buttons, paper clips, woven place mats, tiles, or other textured materials for rubbing
- masking tape
- glue
- scissors

# Procedure

Show your students pictures of temples and the example of the temple rubbing in this lesson.

**1.** Demonstrate how to make a rubbing by placing paper over a textured surface and rubbing over it with the side of a crayon. Rub in one direction only and overlap textures and colors.

**2.** Make rubbings of things found outside, like sidewalks, asphalt, trees, leaves, walls, and poles, or from things found inside, like sandpaper, cheese graters, buttons, paper clips, rubber bands, woven place mats, and tiles.

**3.** Fold the 6" x 9" paper in half, cut out the center leaving a 1" border, and unfold to make a frame.

**4.** Move this frame over your rubbing until you find the most interesting area. Glue the frame to the paper. Trim around the edges.

# Variations

■ Place a 9" x 12" sheet of aluminum foil over an interesting surface like a cheese grater or a collage of objects. Press the foil into the surface to transfer the surface pattern onto the foil. Carefully remove the textured foil and frame it.

■ In place of foil do the above variation using bas-relief paper purchased from a craft store.

# Integration

■ First do rubbings with wax or oil-base crayons. Then paint over the rubbing with water-colors for a resist.

■ For an interesting effect, make rubbings with gold or silver crayon on black butcher paper.

■ Use the rubbing technique and make book covers or stationery.

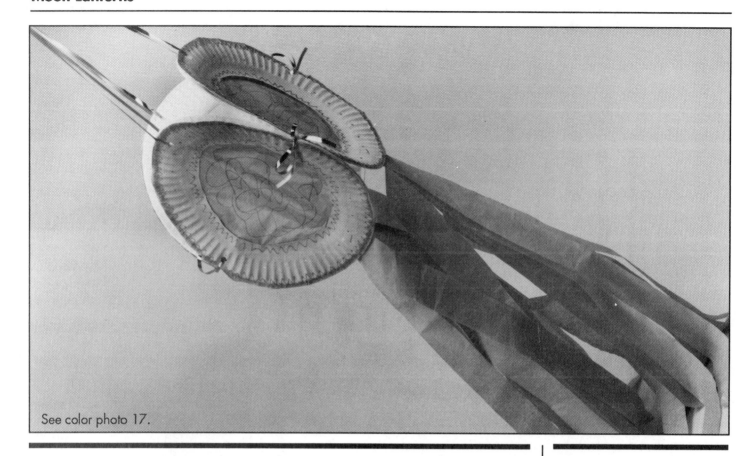

See color photo 17.

# Moon Lanterns

## Materials

- sturdy paper plates (three per student)
- scissors
- pastel-colored tissue paper circles 7" in diameter (three per student)
- tissue paper strips for streamers
- pink tempera paint
- brushes
- yarn or ribbon
- red markers
- tape
- dowels or sticks
- hole punch

**T**et-Trung-thu, the Moon Festival, is an important Vietnamese holiday. A celebration of the moon's beauty, Tet-Trung-thu is observed in late September or early October. The festival originated in the eighth century during the reign of Emperor Minh-Hoang. A legend says that on the fifteenth day of the eighth month of the Chinese lunar calendar, the Emperor took his Empress, Duong Quy Pho, to a beautiful lake, where he composed a poem and read it to her by the light of the full moon. Lantern-making is the festival's most popular activity. On the night of Tet-Trung-thu, children march through the streets carrying their lanterns and singing favorite songs ∎

# Procedure

**1.** Cut the centers out of the three plates. Paint the top side of each plate-ring pink, let dry, and decorate the edges with a red marker.

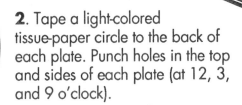

**2.** Tape a light-colored tissue-paper circle to the back of each plate. Punch holes in the top and sides of each plate (at 12, 3, and 9 o'clock).

**3.** Tie the plates together with ribbon or yarn through the holes at 3 and 9 o'clock. Put 12 inches of yarn or ribbon through the top hole of each plate and knot together at the top.

**4.** Add tissue-paper streamers, and attach the lantern to the end of a stick or hang it from the ceiling.

# Variations

■ Use coat hangers bent into a round shape instead of paper plates.

■ Another custom is to buy a flowering branch of the peach tree and place it in a vase for the duration of Tet. Originally this was done to protect homes from demons. Collect some bare tree branches, make pink peach blossoms from tissue paper, and glue them to the branches. Place branches in a simple, elegant vase made by filling a tall, slim bottle with sand.

# Integration

■ Read about other Tet customs.

■ Have your own lantern parade.

■ Read or listen to a Vietnamese folktale.

See color photo 2.

## Materials

- tagboard or stiff paper, 18" x 18" (one per student)
- scissors
- glue
- stapler
- paint, markers, or crayons
- string, yarn, or ribbon
- hole punch

## Notes to the Teacher

Young children can trace a pattern and form the basic hat. Older children can paint the hat or do the other variations.

# Paper Nón lá Hat

**R**ice harvest is a very busy time for the Vietnamese. The rice is brought home and pounded until the grains fall off the stalk. Most of the stalks are used for fuel or building material, but some are set aside to make *nón lá*, the traditional conical hat of the Vietnamese. The straw is turned into sturdy wide-brimmed hats by twisting it into braids, winding the braids in a spiral, and sewing the circular "tows" together. Nón lá are usually neutral in color and have painted or woven designs. Even today, men wear nón lá while working in the fields

## Procedure

**1.** Make a circle with a 7" to 9" radius on the stiff paper. Draw a radius line to the center of the circle. Cut the radius, overlap the edges about 1", and glue or staple them together, forming a slightly cone-shaped hat.

**2.** Paint the hat a natural color, or leave it plain and add a simple flower design. For a chin strap, punch holes on both sides midway up the hat. Pull one piece of yarn or string through the holes, and knot it on the outside.

## Variations

■ Put masking tape strips over the entire surface and stain with a light-colored shoe polish.

■ Place large sheets of newsprint on woven bamboo place mats and do brown crayon rubbings. Glue this paper to the outside of the hats.

■ Fringe strips of crepe paper (brown or yellow) and glue around the hat, starting at the edge of the large circle and overlapping as you go toward the pointed top.

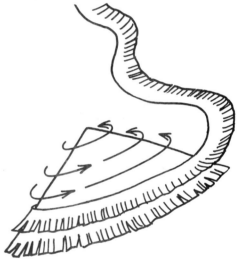

## Integration

■ Just as the Vietnamese often wrote poetry on the inside of their hats, write some poetry about nature on the inside of your hat.

■ Discuss hats and headpieces from different parts of the world. Look at examples of traditional Vietnamese articles of clothing and learn their names.

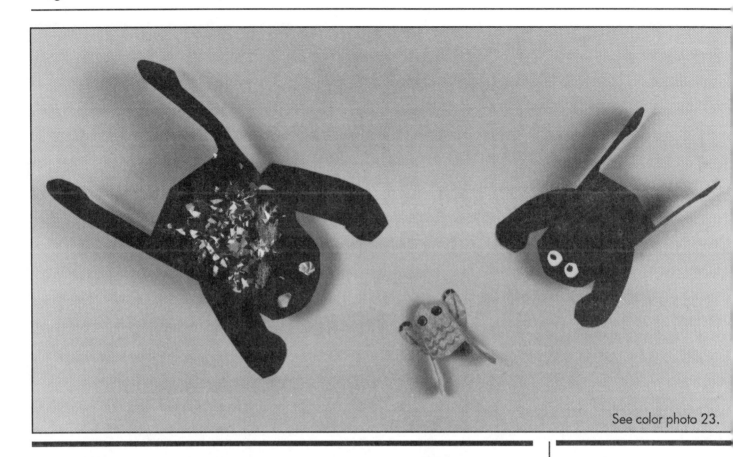

See color photo 23.

# Toy Jumping Frog

**T**hailand—formerly known as Siam—is a wet, tropical land of many rivers.  Frogs abound in its jungles and forests and are favorite pets of Thai children. Children enjoy holding contests to see whose frog can jump the farthest. It is not surprising then that jumping frogs—often in the form of basketry—are a frequent motif of Thai toys and craftwork ▪

## Materials

- ▪ frog pattern on page 98
- ▪ light brown or green construction paper, 6" x 9" (one per student)
- ▪ glue
- ▪ colored markers
- ▪ sequins (optional)
- ▪ scissors

## Teacher Preparation

Prepare frog patterns for each student to trace.

## Procedure

**1.** Trace both pieces of the frog pattern on construction paper, marking points 1A, 2A, and 3A. Cut out.

**2.** Bend in points 1A and 2A on the larger pattern piece so they meet under the body. Glue together.

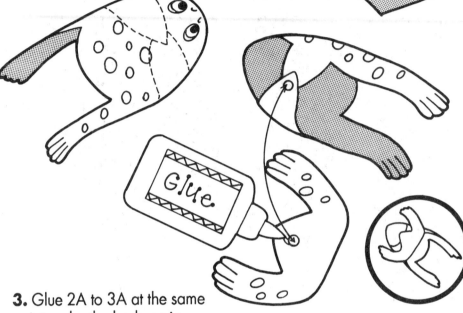

**3.** Glue 2A to 3A at the same point under the body as in step 2. Decorate with markers to resemble a frog; sequins make fun eyes (optional).

**4.** Make your frog jump by pressing one finger *gently* on the frog's back between the legs.

## Variation

■ Make larger frogs in different sizes.

## Integration

■ Find books on frogs and amphibians in the library. Arnold Lobel's stories about Frog and Toad are good fiction choices.

■ Illustrate the life cycle of a frog.

■ Make a chart showing different species of frogs.

■ Find out about the story *The Celebrated Jumping Frog of Calaveras County* by Mark Twain and the annual celebration it inspired in Angels Camp, California. Name your frogs and have a jumping frog contest.

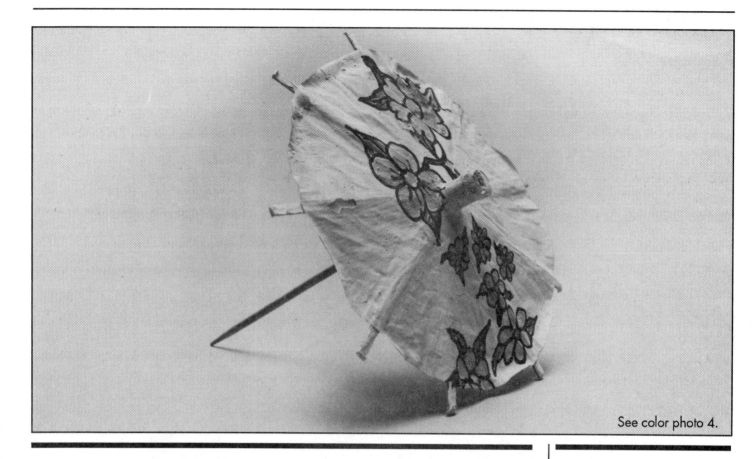

See color photo 4.

# Painted Parasols

## Materials

- small umbrellas available as party favors (one per student)
- white tempera paint
- brushes
- assorted markers
- sequins and glitter (optional)
- glue

**P**arasols plain and fancy are used everywhere in Southeast Asia. When Thais travel by foot,  they use parasols to keep off the sun and rain. Fancy parasols are used at weddings, state functions, and various celebrations. In many Thai villages rice farmers supplement their income by making beautiful painted parasols. They fashion the frames from bamboo, cover them with layers of paper, and paint the completed parasols with festive designs ∎

## Procedure

**1.** Open the umbrellas and paint them white.

**2.** When dry, use markers to create your own festive designs. Glue on sequins or glitter if desired.

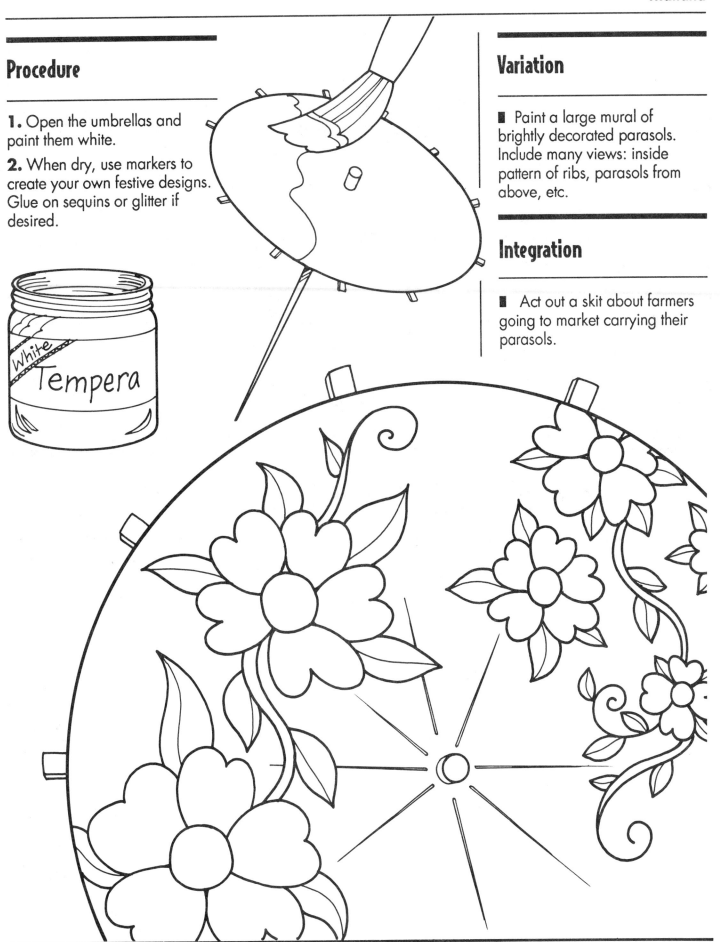

## Variation

■ Paint a large mural of brightly decorated parasols. Include many views: inside pattern of ribs, parasols from above, etc.

## Integration

■ Act out a skit about farmers going to market carrying their parasols.

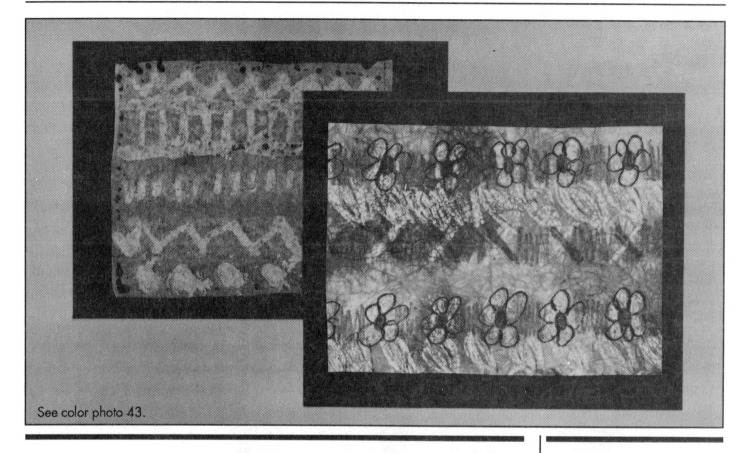

See color photo 43.

# Paper Batik

- white drawing paper or brown wrapping paper, 9" x 12" (one per student)
- crayons
- water
- large bowl
- newspapers
- watercolors
- brushes

For hundreds of years colorful batik sarongs, head scarves, and shawls have been the national dress of Indonesian women. Wishing to imitate the beautiful hand-painted fabrics of southern India, the Javanese developed batik fabric and its wax-resist dye technique. They also invented a tool called the *tjanting* (pronounced "chanting") which enabled them to apply wax in fine lines. Traditional designs use only two colors, a deep indigo blue and a beautiful brown. Today, batik fabrics take their designs from geometric patterns and from natural forms and come in all the colors of the rainbow

## Procedure

**1.** Draw a design on 9" x 12" paper with brightly colored crayons, using heavy pressure to build up a thick layer of wax.

**2.** Dip the paper into a sink or a large bowl of water. Take the paper out and carefully crumple it into a ball.

**3.** Spread the paper out on a bed of newspapers. Brush a contrasting color of watercolor paint over the paper.

**4.** Rinse off the excess watercolor with clear water (over the sink) and allow the paper to dry. The watercolor paint will adhere to the cracks in the wax, giving the effect of batik.

## Variations

■ Use fabric dyes instead of watercolors for a more intense color wash.

■ Use the techniques on fabric, substituting fabric dye.

## Integration

■ Use the "fabrics" to dress dolls in Indonesian-style clothing.

■ Make your own papier-mâché figures and dress them in batiks.

■ Draw geometric designs and create alternating patterns.

See color photo 22 and 44.

# Jeepney Drawing

Filipinos decorate their homes, clothing, cars, and especially their jeepneys with bright colors and intricate designs. *Jeepneys,* canopied vehicles that are half jeep and half taxicab, are used for public transportation. The more pinstriping and the wilder the colors, the more customers a jeepney attracts. Children like to emulate their elders by decorating their own handmade toy jeepneys ▪

## Materials

- jeepney pattern on page 99
- tagboard, 9" x 12" (one per student)
- marking pens (include metallics if available)
- scissors
- black construction paper scraps
- brads
- assorted collage materials
- construction paper canopy fringe

## Teacher Preparation

Teachers prepare enough jeepney patterns for each student to trace.

# Procedure

1. On tagboard, trace the outline of the jeepney pattern with markers. Color and decorate it with pinstripes and collage materials. Make a canopy from fringed paper.

2. Cut out the tagboard jeepney and the spaces under the canopy. (Most jeepneys have only windshields and no other windows.) Cut tires out of black construction paper and attach them with brads to make movable wheels.

# Variations

■ Make the jeepneys three dimensional by decorating two tagboard sides and placing a small box in between.

■ Draw a front view of a the jeepney.

# Integration

■ On a large wall or bulletin board, draw a street with houses and buildings. Attach the jeepneys to create a busy street in Manila.

■ Write a story about owning a jeepney in the Philippines.

■ Study the automobile classified section of a newspaper and write a jeepney advertisement.

See color photo 24.

# Origami Animals

Origami, the art of paper folding, is a favorite pastime of Japanese children. The Japanese have practiced origami for more than ten centuries. Brought to Japan by the Chinese, origami became part of the Doll Festival, where children threw folded paper dolls into the river to drive away evil spirits. The shapes of animals, insects, people, and any number of things can be fashioned from paper. In traditional origami, these objects are made, without cutting or gluing, from a single square sheet of paper ∎

## Materials

- origami paper squares (6" or 10") or any stiff lightweight paper (typing paper, wrapping paper, or shelf paper)

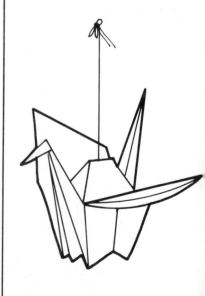

# Procedure

Follow directions for folding paper to make these animals:

## 1. Dog

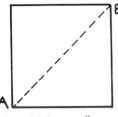

Fold diagonally
along A – B.

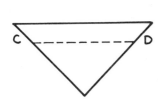

Fold back along C – D.

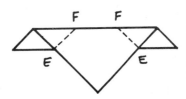

Fold forward along E – F.

Fold back along
G – H and add face.

## 2. Pig

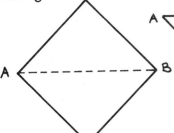

Fold on diagonal.

Fold A and B to C.

Fold ends of ears back
in opposite direction.

Fold up nose of top
sheet and add features.

## 3. Fish

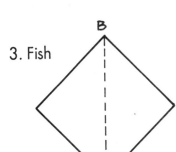

Fold along A – B.

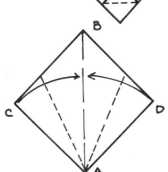

Points C and D
fold into center fold.

Fold down
corner B.

Fold again
along original
A – B centerfold.

Fold up end to create
tail and add details of fish.

# Variation

■ Look through books on
origami and try some of your
favorites designs.

■ Use large squares of
butcher paper for some of
your creations.

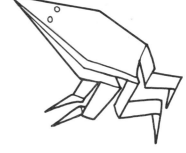

# Integration

■ Glue the origami to a
piece of construction paper.
Draw a background and write
a haiku poem to accompany
the drawing.

■ Make an origami card
for a special occasion in the
coming year.

See color photo 39.

# Spoon Dolls

## Materials

- kimono pattern on page 103
- white plastic spoons (one per student)
- gift wrapping paper, preferably with Japanese patterns
- glue
- permanent markers
- paper strip for obi sash, (one per student) 1" x 7" in a plain or contrasting pattern
- scissors
- assorted paper scraps

## Teacher Preparation

Prepare a kimono pattern for each student to trace.

**T**here are several types of Japanese dolls: Wooden *kokeshi* dolls have a movable head that squeaks when it is turned, but no arms or legs. *Daruma* dolls, also without legs or arms, are designed to roll and right themselves. Used during Japanese New Year, they symbolize man's ability to recover from adverstiy. *Daire-sama* dolls, representing the Japanese emperor and empress, are displayed on Girl's Day. Spoon dolls are used as decorations. A face is painted on the spoon and the doll is dressed in paper costumes ▪

## Procedure

**1.** Fold the gift wrapping paper. Trace the kimono pattern and cut it out.

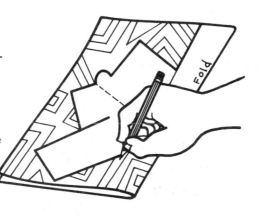

**2.** With markers, draw a simple face on the back of the plastic spoon. Dress the spoon with the kimono piece. Glue it in place if you don't want to change clothing.

**3.** For the obi, or sash, wrap the 1" x 7" strip of paper around the kimono and glue. Fold the arms in for a girl. Make a flower or a small fan from paper scraps for the girl. Leave the arms extended for a boy. Make a small kite from scraps for the boy to hold.

## Variations

■ Cut umbrella shapes out of paper and attach to toothpicks, or purchase tiny umbrellas to add to the dolls.

■ Make more costumes if you want to change the doll's clothing.

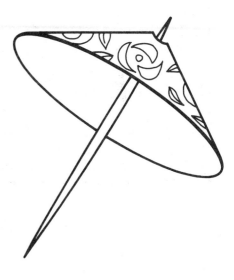

## Integration

■ Have a Doll Day at school and bring in your collections.

■ Debate the pros and cons of celebrating a children's doll day here in this country.

■ Read about the history of dolls in the encyclopedia or in another reference book.

See color photo 11.

## Materials

- long piece of brown butcher paper
- large squares of white butcher paper, 24" x 24" (one per student)
- scissors
- glue

# Paper Alpana

**D**iwali, India's Festival of Lights, is celebrated in October or November. It commemorates the homecoming of the epic hero Rama and the welcome given him by Lakshimi, the goddess of good fortune. During Diwali thousands of lamps are placed on rooftops, along roads, and inside and outside of houses to ensure a visit by Lakshimi. Indian women also create *alpanas*—good luck designs made from rice flour and colored powder—on the ground in front of their doorways, on the steps, and on porches. A flour mixture is dripped through the fingers into the pattern sketched on the ground or floor. The designs may either be abstract or in traditional patterns such as paisley ▌

## Procedure

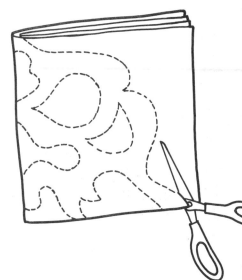

**1.** Fold the large square of white butcher paper in half and fold it in half again. (Other folds may also be made if you have sharp scissors.)

**2.** Make a large lacy open design by cutting out pieces from all folds and all edges. Open carefully when finished.

**3.** Glue the designs to the brown paper, making sure the edges are completely attached.

**4.** Display all the class alpanas glued to the butcher paper.

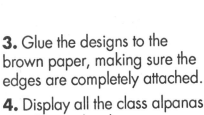

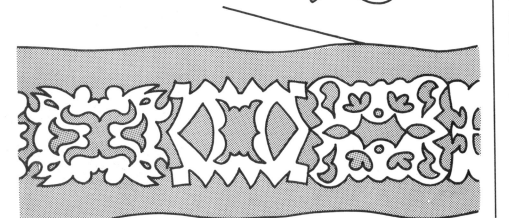

## Variations

■ Decorate the school grounds or sidewalks with colored chalk designs.

■ Decorate graham crackers with cake icing alpanas.

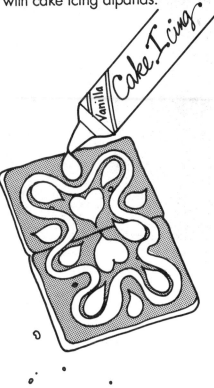

## Integration

■ Compare and contrast alpana paintings with sand paintings.

■ Make alpanas of different sizes to attach to different places; for example, greeting cards, tablecloths, and medallions.

■ Make a wish for yourself, your family, your school, your country, and the world. Write one wish on each alpana design.

See color photos 15 and 32.

## Materials

- white T-shirts or white cotton cloth, washed (one per student)
- rubber bands
- cold water dyes (special dyes for tie-dyeing are available at craft stores)
- scissors
- wooden spoons
- rubber gloves
- buckets or large bowls

## Teacher Preparation

Prepare dye according to package directions in large bowls or buckets. Prepare a place to hang the material while it dries. Experiment with different kinds of tying and dyeing. Be sure children wear old clothes and cover-ups.

# Tie-dyeing

India has the longest continuous history of fabric decoration of any country on earth. More than 5,000 years ago, Indians carved stamps that produced designs when rolled over cloth. After the cylinder method came block printing, wax-resist, and tie-dyeing. Craft workers wove their own fabric and made their dyes from natural substances like fruit, bark, roots, and flowers. Mud was used to fix the colors. Many Indian textile inventions have been copied by other cultures. One such is tie-dyeing, which was practiced in India as long ago as 700 B.C. The Indian words for tie-dyeing are *mahaju* or *schiboris* ∎

## Procedure

**1.** Gather up areas of shirt or cloth at random and twist rubber bands tightly around them.

**2.** Place the shirt or cloth in buckets or large bowls of dye, prepared from package directions, and stir. Leave the fabric in the dye for longer than the time suggested.

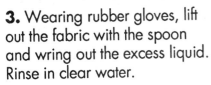

Dye bucket

**3.** Wearing rubber gloves, lift out the fabric with the spoon and wring out the excess liquid. Rinse in clear water.

**4.** Cut the rubber bands and spread the fabric out to dry.

Rinse bucket

## Variations

■ Dye different parts of the fabric in different colors. Overlap colors in other places. After you take off the rubber bands, twist rubber bands around other areas of the fabric then dip the fabric into a darker color.

## Integration

■ Try other Indian methods of decorating fabrics: stamping, embroidery, batik, and the addition of mirrors to fabrics.

■ Try dyeing fabrics with natural dyes made from spinach or red cabbage.

■ Read *The Magic Cooking Pot* by Faith M. Towle, and act out your favorite part.

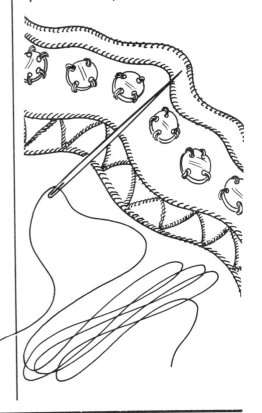

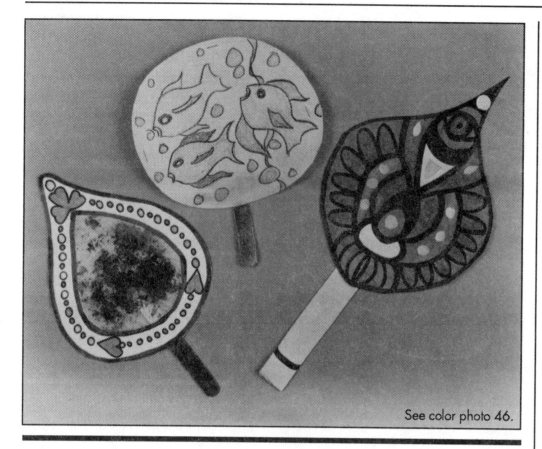

See color photo 46.

## Materials

- fan pattern on page 100
- lightweight cardboard pieces, 9" x 9" square (2 per student)
- wax paper pieces, 8" x 8" square (2 per student)
- small pieces of colored tissue paper
- crayon shavings
- tongue depressors or craft sticks
- crayons
- paint
- iron
- glue
- stapler
- scissors

# Paper Fan

## Teacher Preparation

Prepare a fan pattern for each student to trace.

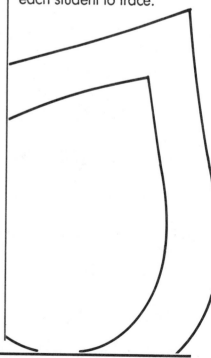

In Korea as elsewhere in Asia, fans are both useful and decorative. Korean screen and folding fans come in many colors and display such familiar motifs as orchids, peach blossoms, lotus flowers, butterflies, and herons. Koreans use large round fans as sun screens and banana leaf fans as ornaments. At traditional weddings, the bridegroom holds a blue fan and the bride screens her face with a red fan made of silk and sewn with pearls ▪

## Procedure

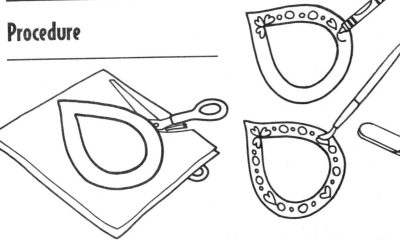

**1.** Trace and cut out two fan frames from lightweight cardboard. With crayons or paint, color the outside of the frames and both sides of the craft stick handle.

**2.** Place colored tissue paper and/or crayon shavings between the two pieces of wax paper, and press with a warm iron.

**3.** Place wax paper and one end of the craft stick handle between the two frames. Staple and glue the frames together.

**4.** Trim off excess wax paper.

## Variations

■ Make a flat fan decorated with the symbol that stands for the balance and unity in nature. Color the design with paint or markers.

■ Make a folding fan from fancy wallpaper and trim it with feathers.

## Integration

■ Listen to traditional Korean music and fan yourself while drinking a cup of tea.

■ Study the meaning of the *talguk*, or *yin-yang* symbol, which stands for the universe in perfect balance. It is the symbol on the North Korean flag.

■ Make a fan decorated with flowers or birds.

See color photo 21.

# Decorative Bird Kite

**K**oreans have many traditions involving kites. When a Korean child asks for toys, his mother ties a list of the toys to the tail of a kite. By flying this kite the child tells the gods what he wants. Similarly, to celebrate the new year some Koreans write a list of their year's troubles on the tail of a bird-shaped kite and fly it as high and as long as possible before releasing it. In this way, the kite-flier frees himself of his troubles and starts the new year afresh ▪

## Materials

- wood or dowels, 7½" and 14" (for each student)
- bird-kite pattern on page 101
- tissue paper, 9" x 16" (one per student)
- scissors
- glue
- markers
- string

## Teacher Preparation

Prepare a bird kite pattern for each student to trace. Cut wood or dowels in 7½" pieces and 14" pieces, one of each size for each student.

## Procedure

**1.** Glue sticks together forming a "T" shape. Allow to dry thoroughly.

**2.** Fold the tissue paper and trace the bird pattern. Cut it out.

**3.** Attach the wood frame to the tissue with glue at wing tips and tail. Draw eyes on the bird.

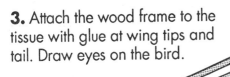

*Glue*

*Glue*

**4.** Attach string to the tail and use tissue paper scraps to create tail bows.

## Variations

■ Try making simple kites in other shapes.

■ Design and make a kite. See if it will fly.

## Integration

■ Celebrate the Korean New Year sometime in February. Have students dress in their best clothes. When they come to school, have them bow to their teacher. The teacher, in turn, should hand out a small gift. Rice cakes dipped in honey could be served. Later, kites with messages can be flown and released. Because the number nine is believed to bring good luck, think of something to do nine times, such as hopping on one foot nine times or snapping one's fingers nine times.

See color photo 1.

# Dragon Hat

## Materials

- green construction paper, 12" x 18" (one per student)
- green construction paper, 6" x 12" (one per student)
- scissors
- glue
- stapler
- bright paper scraps
- something gold: glitter, paint, marker, or paper scraps

**T**he dragon is an age-old Chinese symbol. Instead of being a fearsome creature, the dragon is a symbol of good fortune, and dragon motifs appear on everything from clothing to dishes, toys, and walls. During Chinese New Year the dragon's appearance is the eagerly awaited finale to the holiday parade. The highly decorated dragon is carried by the bravest and strongest young men. Amid the popping of firecrackers and the laughter of onlookers, the dragon weaves down the street, smoke streaming from its nostrils, bringing good luck to all who see it ■

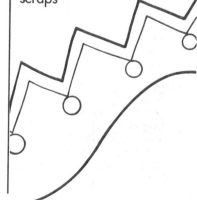

## Procedure

**1.** Cut the large piece of green paper in half with a large zig-zag cut.

**2.** Glue or staple the paper together. Wrap this strip around your head, overlap it to fit, and draw a line. Remove the strip from your head and staple.

**3.** Cut the 6" x 12" green paper diagonally with a zigzag cut as shown. Accordion-fold and glue one of these pieces to the end of the dragon's body. Discard the second piece or share it with a friend.

**4.** Add dragon features to the front using bright paper scraps and decorate with gold. Accordion-fold the tailpiece.

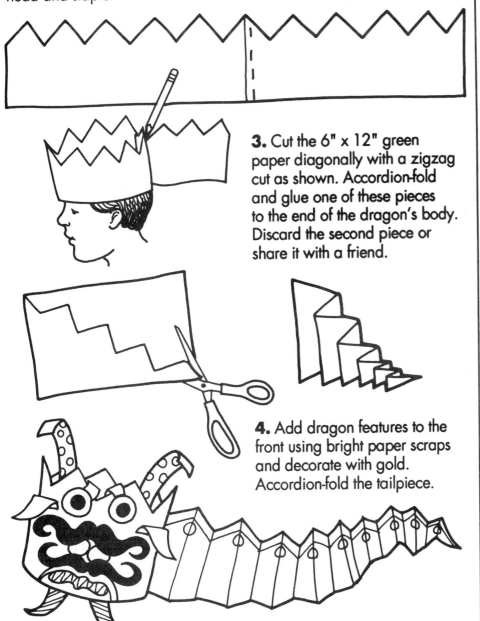

## Variations

■ Make a class dragon by having each member of the class decorate a paper plate. One plate should show the head. String the plates together with knotted string.

■ Make dragon kites.

## Integration

■ Make a list of New Year's resolutions for the class.

■ Celebrate the Chinese New Year with a parade of many dragons.

■ Look at a Chinese zodiac calendar and find out what the animal symbol is for the year.

■ Find out the Chinese symbol and horoscope for the year you were born.

See color photo 45.

# Butterfly Paper Cut

**F**or centuries paper cutting has been a popular Chinese craft. Cutouts were hung on doors to celebrate the 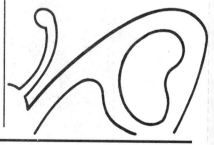 new year and served as window coverings before glass windows came into use. Elaborate fish were placed on the ceilings of children's rooms to protect the children as they slept. Made with scissors or with chisels, paper cuts come in bright colors and represent such things as flowers, birds, trees, and animals. Red, the most popular color, stands for loyalty, integrity, and good luck ∎

## Materials

- butterfly pattern page 102
- red and black construction paper, 9" x 12"
- sharp scissors
- glue
- paper punch
- pencil

## Teacher Preparation

Prepare a butterfly pattern for each student to trace.

## Procedure

**1.** Fold the black paper in half. Use your own design or trace the pattern and cut out a butterfly shape.

**2.** Using a paper punch to start cuts in areas away from the fold, cut on the heavy black lines to make wings.

## Variations

■ Glue the butterfly to a paper plate and spray it with lacquer or clear plastic glaze. (Lacquerware is also a Chinese art form.)

■ Look at examples of Chinese paper cuts and try making different paper-cut designs like fish, flowers, birds, animals, or trees.

■ Do crayon rubbings of some of your paper cuts.

**3.** Open the paper carefully, and glue the butterfly to the red paper.

## Integration

■ Compare and contrast Chinese paper cuts with those from Scandinavia, Mexico, and Israel.

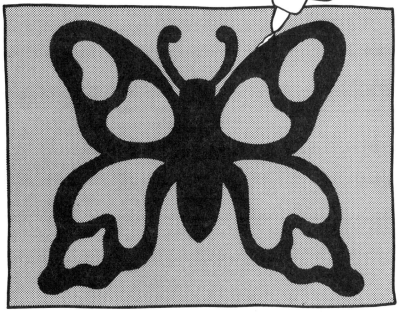

# Literature Selections for North America

## Mexico

Aardema, Verna. *Pedro and the Padre: A Tale From Jalisco, Mexico*. Dial, 1991.

_____. *Borreguita and the Coyote: A Tale From Ayutla, Mexico*. Knopf, 1991.

Behrens, June. *Fiesta! Ethnic Traditional Holidays*. Childrens Press, 1978.

Blanco, Alberto. *The Desert Mermaid*. Childrens Press, 1992.

Blackmore, Vivian. *Why Corn Is Golden*. Little, Brown, 1984.

Coronado, Rosa. *Cooking the Mexican Way*. Lerner, 1982.

Delacre, Lulu. *Arroz Con Leche: Popular Songs and Rhymes From Latin America*. Scholastic, 1989.

dePaola, Tomie. *The Lady of Guadalupe*. Holiday, 1980.

Fisher, Leonard Everett. *Pyramid of the Sun, Pyramid of the Moon*. Macmillan, 1989.

Haskins, Jim. *Count Your Way Through Mexico*. Carolrhoda, 1988.

Inizarry, Carmen. *Passport to Mexico*. Franklin Watts, 1987.

Lattimore, Deborah Nourse. *The Flame of Peace: A Tale of the Aztecs*. HarperCollins, 1987.

Lewis, Richard. *All of You Was Singing*. Atheneum, 1991.

Lewis, Thomas P. *Hill of Fire*. HarperCollins, 1971.

Lye, Keith. *Take a Trip to Mexico*. Franklin Watts, 1982.

Miller, Edna. *The Jumping Bean*. Prentice Hall, 1979.

Rohmer, Harriet. *The Legend of Food Mountain*. Childrens Press, 1988.

Rolans, Donna. *Grandfather's Stories From Mexico*. Educational Activities, 1986.

Somonte, Carlos. *We Live in Mexico*. Watts, 1985.

Tompert, Ann. *The Silver Whistle*. Macmillan, 1988.

Williams, Vera B. *Music, Music for Everyone*. Greenwillow, 1984.

Wisiniewski, David. *Rain Player*. Clarion Books, 1991.

## United States and Canada

Aliki. *Corn Is Maize: The Gift of the Indians*. HarperCollins, 1976.

Baker, Olaf. *Where the Buffaloes Begin*. Viking, 1989.

Baylor, Byrd. *When Clay Sings*. Scribners, 1972.

_____. *The Desert Is Theirs*. Scribners, 1975.

Behrens, June. *Powwow: Festivals and Holidays*. Childrens Press, 1983.

Blood, Charles and Martin Link. *The Goat in the Rug*. Four Winds Press, 1976.

Brown, Virginia P. *World of the Southern Indians*. Beechwood Books, 1983.

Bruchac, Joseph, and Jonathan London. *Thirteen Moons on Turtle's Back: A Native American Year of the Moons*. Philomel, 1992.

Cleaver, Elizabeth. *The Fire Starter*. Oxford University Press, 1979.

Climo, Shirley. *King of the Birds*. HarperCollins/Crowell, 1988.

Cohen, Caron Lee. *The Mud Pony*. Scholastic, 1988.

Cohlene, Terri. *Turquoise Boy: A Navajo Legend*. Troll, 1990.

_____. *Clamshell Boy: A Makah Legend*. Watermill Press, 1990.

dePaola, Tomie. *The Legend of the Bluebonnet*. Putnam, 1983.

Dixon, Sarah and Peter Dixon. *Children, Families, and the Sea*. Cypress, 1979.

Ekoomiak, Normee. *Artic Memories*. Henry Holt, 1992.

Fradin, Dennis. *Alaska: In Words and Pictures*. Childrens Press, 1977.

Fritz, Jean. *The Double Life of Pocahontas*. Putnam, 1983.

Garbarino, Merwyn S. *The Seminole*. Chelsea House, 1989.

George, Jean Craighead. *The Talking Earth*. HarperCollins, 1983.

Gill, Shelley. *Alaska's Three Bears*. Paws IV Publishing, 1992.

Gobel, Paul. *Buffalo Woman*. Macmillan, 1984.

_____. *Iktomi and the Boulder: A Plains Indian Story*. Watts, 1988.

Graymont, Barbara. *The Iroquois*. Chelsea House, 1989.

Heady, Eleanor. *Sage Smoke*. Silver Burdette Press, 1993.

Joosse, Barbara M. *Mama, Do You Love Me?* Chronicle Books, 1991.

Keehn, Sally. *I Am Regina*. Philomel, 1991.

Kreeger, Charlene. The *Alaska ABC Book*. Paws IV Publishing, 1978.

_____. *Kiana's Iditarod*. Paws IV Publishing, 1984.

Lacapa, Michael. *The Flute Player: An Apache Folktale*. Northland, 1990.

Lepthien, Emilie U. *The Choctaw*. Childrens Press, 1987.

Martin, Bill Jr. *Knots on a Counting Rope*. Henry Holt, 1987.

Moroney, Lynn. *Baby Rattlesnake*. Childrens Press, 1989.

Opinski, Alice. *The Navajo*. Childrens Press, 1987.

Ortiz, Simon. *The People Shall Continue*. Childrens Press, 1988.

San Souci, Robert D. *Song of Sedna*. Doubleday, 1989.

_____. *The Legend of Scarface*. Doubleday, 1987.

*Multicultural Art Activities*

# North American Art

The Native Americans who inhabited almost all of the North American continent developed arts and crafts that have enriched the modern cultures of Canada, the United States, and Mexico. Native American art is as varied as the tribes that create it, yet all of it shows a reverence for nature and a pride of workmanship. Long before Columbus, the Indians of North America were skilled artists and craftsmen, adept at carving, painting, metal-working, weaving, and pottery making.

The arts of Mexico are a rich blend of European and native traditions. Typified by vivid colors, bold patterns, and motifs of both European and Indian origin, they reflect the Mexico of yesterday and today.

See color photo 16.

# Paper Bag Piñata

## Materials

- paper lunch bag (one per student)
- old newspapers
- wrapped hard candies or small toys (optional)
- strips of brightly colored tissue paper, 4" wide
- strips of brightly colored tissue paper, 1" wide
- glue
- string, twine, or a shoe-lace, 24" long (one per student)
- scissors
- hole punch

**M**exicans celebrate their religious and historical holidays with colorful fiestas. An important part of these celebrations is the ▣ breaking of a decorated container called a *piñata*, a tradition that goes back more than 400 years to the days of the first Spaniards. The piñata symbolizes the love of possessions, and the treats inside represent blessings. When the piñata is broken with "the stick of goodness," the love of worldly goods is destroyed and blessings are showered on the merrymakers. Made around a thin *olla* (oh-yah), or 👹 clay pot, piñatas must be durable enough to pull up and down with a rope, yet fragile 🐍 enough to shatter after several blows ∎

## Procedure

**1.** Stuff the paper bag about ⅔ full with crumpled newspaper. Add candies or small toys if desired. Fold about 2" of the top of the bag to the outside.

**2.** Fringe the four-inch-wide tissue paper strips by cutting every 1".

**3.** Glue the uncut edge of the tissue strips around the bag, starting from the bottom of the bag and going to the top. Overlap the fringed edges as you go.

Glue

**4.** Punch holes around the top edge of the bag every 1". Thread a twine or shoestring through the holes and pull to gather the top closed. Tie the bag closed and use the remaining string to hang the piñata.

**5.** Glue the one-inch-wide strips of tissue paper to the bottom of the bag as streamers.

## Variations

■ Use the paper bag for the body and add other parts to make an animal.

■ Make piñatas from two paper plates stapled together or from paper cups or empty milk cartons. Add simple cut out shapes to make birds, sombreros or other objects. Fringe tissue paper strips and glue them around these shapes.

## Integration

■ Learn more about Cinco de Mayo or the Christmas posadas celebration in Mexico. Have a posada procession or Cinco de Mayo parade from room to room, and invite another class to break a piñata with you.
■ Learn a Mexican song to sing to your guests.

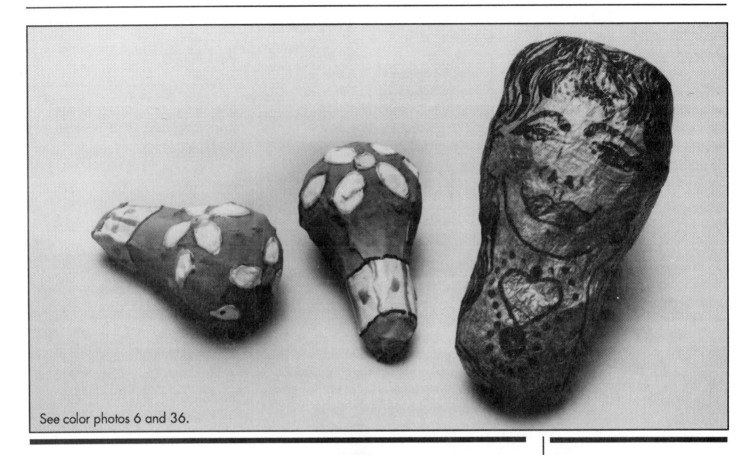

See color photos 6 and 36.

# Maracas

## Materials

- empty plastic prescription drug containers or film cans (2 for each student)
- dried beans or small pebbles
- newspaper sheets
- newspaper, paper towel, or other absorbent paper strips, 1" x 3"
- masking tape
- flour and water mixed to the consistency of a creamy gravy (glue mixture)
- tempera paints
- paint brushes

## Teacher Preparation

Prepare glue mixture and tear paper strips.

*M*aracas are a common percussion instrument used to accompany Mexican music. Originally made from dried gourds in which the seeds provide the rattle, these popular instruments can be made from many different materials, including papier-mâché. Spanish and French colonists introduced Mexico to the art of papier-mâché—a light, strong molding material made of paper and glue. A flourishing craft in Mexico today, Mexican papier-mâché is now exported to France, Switzerland, Spain, and the United States. Talented Mexican artisans fashion everything from tiny birds and flowers to large pieces of furniture from this versatile medium ∎

## Procedure

**1.** Place three or four beans or pebbles in the plastic container. Put the container in the center of a half sheet of newspaper. (Additional crumpled paper can be added around the container if a larger maraca head is desired.) Gather together the newspaper around the container at the bottom. Twist the paper and tape it to hold together for a handle.

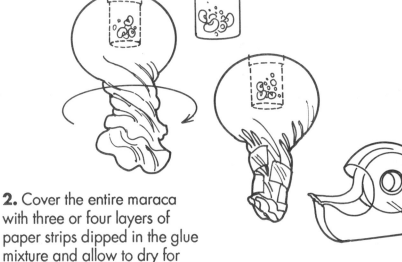

**2.** Cover the entire maraca with three or four layers of paper strips dipped in the glue mixture and allow to dry for several days.

**3.** Paint with bright colors.

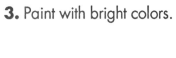

## Variations

■ Old picture frames or small boxes may be covered with papier-mâché.

■ Instead of painting the maraca, glue colored tissue paper over the papier-mâché for interesting color combinations and texture.

## Integration

■ Play Mexican music and accompany it with the maracas.

See color photo 27.

# Paper Tree of Life

## Materials

- tree of life pattern, page 105
- assorted colors of construction paper, 12" x 18" (one per student)
- black construction paper, 12" x 18" (one per student)
- scraps of brightly colored construction paper
- scissors
- glue

## Teacher Preparation

Prepare the tree of life pattern for each student to trace. Older students can make their own more intricate designs.

The tree of life, or *arbol de la vida*, a motif which originated in the Middle ⬚⬚ East, was brought to Spain by the Moors. The Spanish reinterpreted the symbol according to Christian beliefs and introduced it to Mexico. A popular subject among the potters of the Indian village of Metepec, the tree of life is a candle-bearing sculpture usually made of brightly painted clay and adorned with the shapes of whimsical flowers, birds, and animals. Traditionally, the Mexican tree of life was used as a candleholder in church ceremonies. ∎

## Procedure

**1.** Fold the 12" x 18" colored paper in half and trace the fanciful tree of life candleholder from the pattern.

**2.** Cut it out and glue it to the black construction paper.

**3.** Think of an interesting theme, such as animals, trees, or events in your life. Cut out symbols of these and glue them onto the branches of the candleholder. Include candles and flames.

## Variation

■ The tree of life usually has a central theme that is religious, patriotic, or inspired by nature. Design a class tree of life from a theme chosen by the children. Paint it on butcher paper, using fluorescent paint.

## Integration

■ Write a story to go along with your creation; or listen to a Mexican folktale before making your "trees," and depict the story.

■ Research your own family tree and make a tree of life to represent your findings.

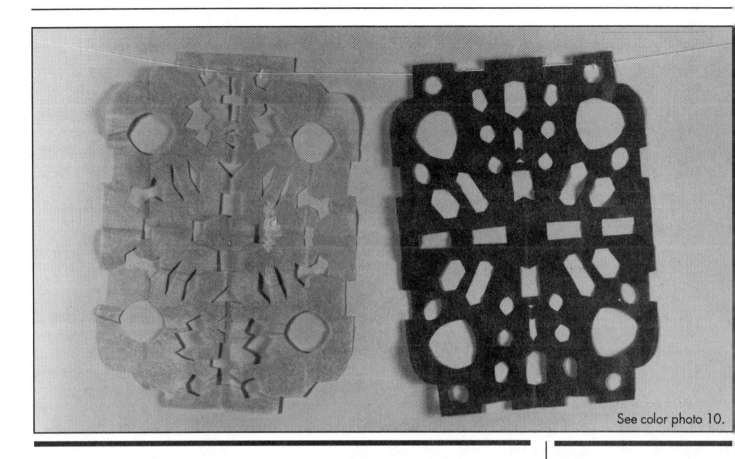

See color photo 10.

# Fiesta Banner

**N**o fiesta is complete without music, dancing, flowers, and colorful decorations. Colorful paper banners are popular fiesta decorations. Cut from different colors of tissue paper and strung on a string, banners festoon the streets of small towns and flutter above banquet tables and restaurant patios. They are also placed on tables and, for the Day of the Dead, on family altars. Created by skilled artists who stack many layers of paper and use sharp instruments to punch out the designs, each banner is unique. Religious symbols are common motifs as are images from nature, such as birds, animals, flowers, and butterflies ▪

## Materials

- assorted colors of tissue paper, 18" x 24" (one per student)
- scissors
- tape
- string

## Notes to the Teacher

To make the cutting easier, younger children can make fewer folds. You may want students to draw designs on the folded rectangle for you to approve before cutting.

12.

13.

14.

14.

15.

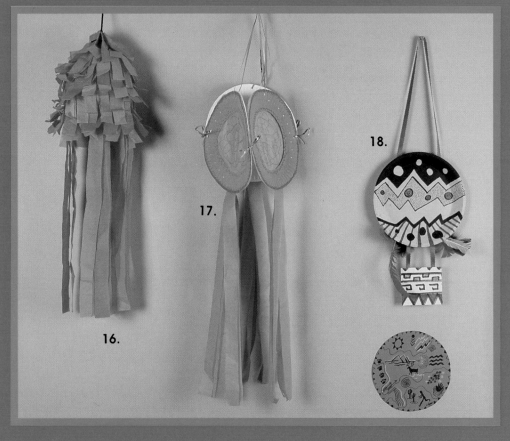

16.

17.

18.

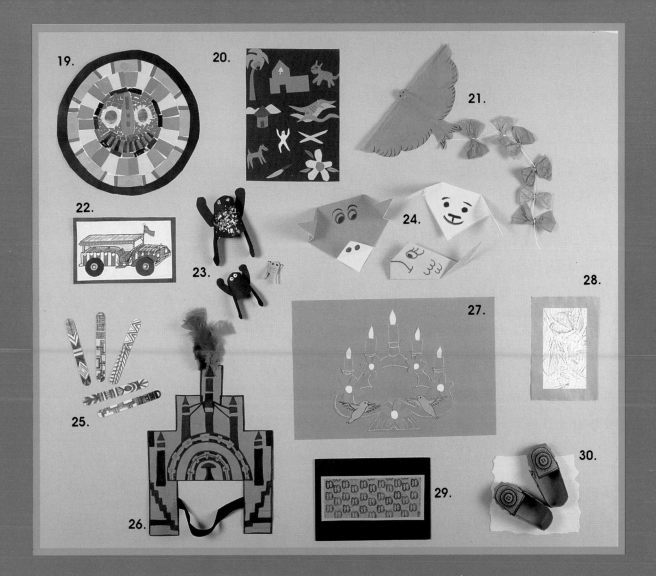

37.

41.

39.

40.

38.

42.

43.

44.

40.

43.

45.

46.

47.

48.

49.

49.

## Procedure

**1.** Fold the paper in half at least five times.

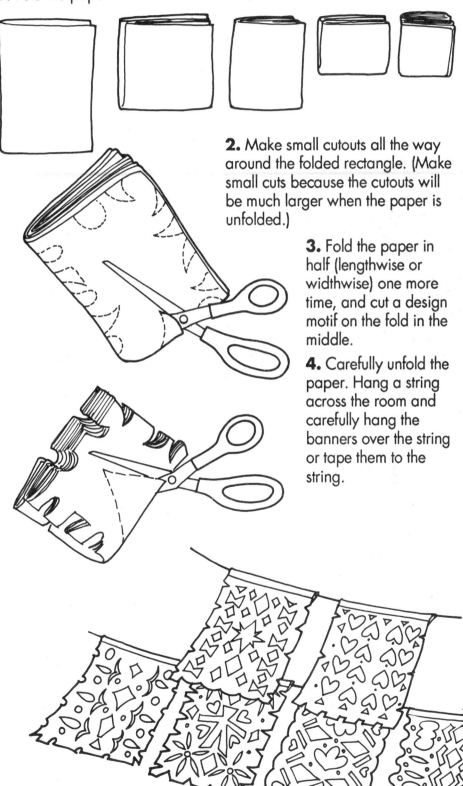

**2.** Make small cutouts all the way around the folded rectangle. (Make small cuts because the cutouts will be much larger when the paper is unfolded.)

**3.** Fold the paper in half (lengthwise or widthwise) one more time, and cut a design motif on the fold in the middle.

**4.** Carefully unfold the paper. Hang a string across the room and carefully hang the banners over the string or tape them to the string.

## Variations

■ Place banners on top of a contrasting color of tissue or butcher paper, laminate them, and give them as gifts or use them to make covers for reports about Mexico.

## Integration

■ Make green, white, and red banners for Cinco de Mayo or Mexican Independence Day. Decorate your room for a party. Serve Mexican snacks, play Mexican music, and do a Mexican dance.

See color photo 34.

## Materials

- moist pottery clay ball, about 2" to 3" in diameter (one per student)
- ceramic underglazes
- brushes
- kiln
- small containers of water

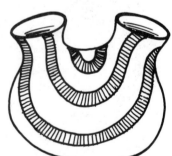

# Clay Pinch Pot

Long ago the native peoples of Mexico [symbols] discovered that certain [symbol] kinds of earth, or clay, could be shaped into pottery. Potters painted their wares with geometric figures, designs from nature, and pictographic symbols from religion and myth. [symbol] Today, pottery is often made by entire families for sale in the marketplace. Mexican terracotta, or baked clay pottery, is very breakable, reflecting the Indian belief that pots should [symbol] be used for a certain number of years, [symbol] then thrown against rocks and destroyed. It was considered a bad omen if a pot did not break readily and release its spirit ∎

# Procedure

**1.** Wedge the clay (throw it down on a hard surface several times to remove air bubbles) and knead it like dough.

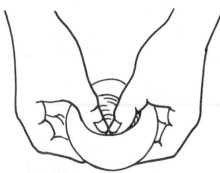
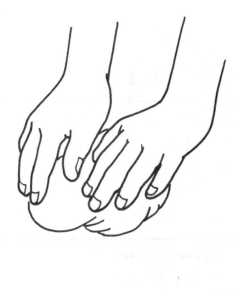

**2.** Pat and smooth the clay into a ball and push both thumbs together into the middle. Shape a bowl by pulling the sides out from the center and pinching with the fingers. Don't pinch the edges too thin. Turn the bowl frequently so that the sides remain the same thickness.

**3.** Dip your fingers into water and smooth out any cracks in the surface of the pot. Let the pot dry several days.

**4.** Look at examples of Mexican pottery, and paint a design with underglaze that is similar to the examples.

**5.** Fire according to manufacturer's directions.

# Variation

■ Instead of using underglaze, fire the container and paint it with a reddish-brown tempera paint. When the paint is dry, add a design in a second color. Spray with ceramic sealer or lacquer if desired.

# Integration

■ Make a list of things your little pot could hold such as rings, pennies, or marbles.

■ Write a poem about the pot.

My little pot holds lots of things:
Marbles
Pennies
Gum and
Rings!

See color photo 3.

# Paper Flowers

## Materials

- assorted colors of tissue paper, 6" x 9" (six sheets per student)
- scissors
- pipe cleaners (one per student)

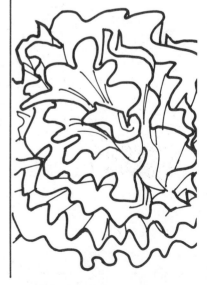

**W**hile the village of Xochimilco has changed greatly since the days of the Aztecs, it is still the Place of Flowers. When the Aztecs moved to the Valley of Mexico, a region of lakes and marshes, they increased the land available for cultivation by creating floating gardens. On rafts covered with soil they grew fruits, vegetables, and flowers. In time, these floating gardens put down roots and became islands anchored to the lake bed. Today, all that remains of the floating gardens of Xochimilco are canals thronged with the flower-bedecked boats of vendors. The paper flowers that decorate them are a favorite souvenir of tourists ▮

# Procedure

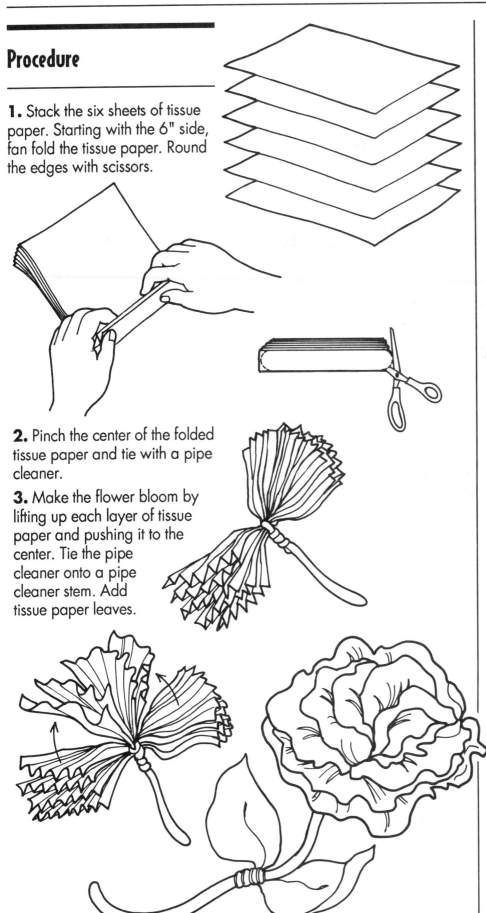

**1.** Stack the six sheets of tissue paper. Starting with the 6" side, fan fold the tissue paper. Round the edges with scissors.

**2.** Pinch the center of the folded tissue paper and tie with a pipe cleaner.

**3.** Make the flower bloom by lifting up each layer of tissue paper and pushing it to the center. Tie the pipe cleaner onto a pipe cleaner stem. Add tissue paper leaves.

# Variations

■ Use colored facial tissues or colored paper napkins instead of tissue.

■ Add glitter and perfume to the flowers.

■ Make a vase for your flowers.

# Integration

■ Wear the flowers and perform a Mexican dance.

■ Set up a Mexican market and practice simple Spanish phrases while buying, selling, and trading your Mexican flowers.

■ Cook a simple Mexican meal and use your flowers to decorate the table.

■ Read about how flowers got their names in *Why Corn Is Golden*, a collection of ancient Mexican legends about plants, adapted by Vivian Blackmore.

See color photo 31.

# Ojo de Dios

## Materials

- sticks (straight branches, dowels, skewers, or craft sticks) 2 per student
- yarn or raffia in bright colors
- glue

**T**he *ojo de dios*, or god's eye, a simple weaving made across two sticks, is thought to have originated with the  Huichol Indians of Jalisco. The Huichol call their god's eyes *sikuli*, which means "the power to see and understand things unknown." Hung in a child's hair or on the walls of homes, or tied to the ends of arrows, the sikuli's main purpose is to ensure children a long and healthy life. When a child is born, the central eye is woven by the father. Then one eye is added for every year of the child's life until the youngster reaches the age of five. The resulting design in the shape of a cross symbolizes the four elements of earth, air, fire, and water ∎

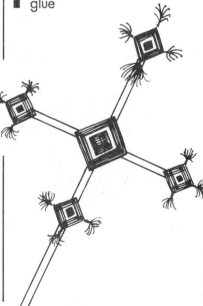

# Procedure

**1.** Cross the sticks in the middle. Glue or tie them together securely at a 90° angle. Mark the end of each stick A, B, C, and D.

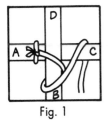

Fig. 1

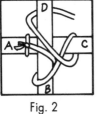

Fig. 2

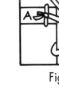

Fig. 3

**2.** Tie the yarn around stick A. Then wind the yarn once around stick B. (fig. 1) Proceed in the same manner with C and D. (fig. 2)

**3.** Continue in this manner until you reach the ends of the sticks. (fig. 3) Tie the end of the yarn and tuck it in. Add yarn tassels if desired.

# Variations

■ For a three-dimensional effect, wind yarn around the sticks in the opposite direction and reverse the rotation of the sticks.

■ Make different sizes of ojos by using a variety of stick sizes.

■ Experiment with different colors of yarn perhaps using a different color for each direction. Tie each new color to the end of the original color in the back.

# Integration

■ Decorate the room with god's eyes, maracas (pages 60–61), flowers (pages 68–69), and piñatas (page 58–59). Prepare foods and have a Mexican fiesta.

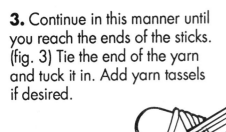

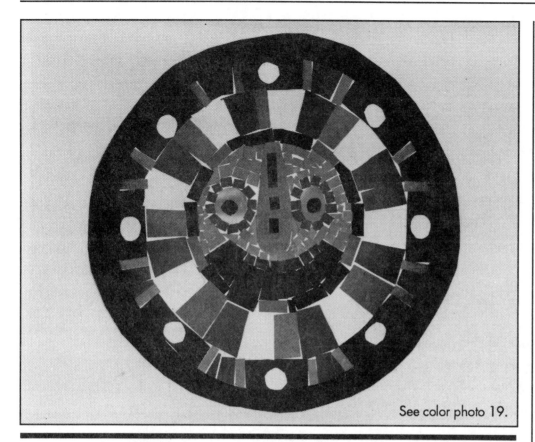

See color photo 19.

## Materials

- sun god pattern on page 104
- variety of paper scraps, including colorful magazine pages
- tagboard or a paper plate (one per student)
- glue
- black markers or black crayons
- spray varnish or fixative (optional)
- scissors

## Teacher Preparation

Prepare a sun god pattern for each student to glue on the tagboard or paper plate. This sun god pattern can be simplified for younger children if necessary. Older students can research the Aztec calendar and make their own with more intricate and perhaps authentic designs if desired.

# Mosaic Sun God

**T**he Aztecs, who considered themselves "the People of the Sun," worshipped [icon] many gods and goddesses including the sun god, Huitzilopochtli, also referred to as Tonatiuh. The Aztecs believed that without rituals [icon] (in many cases involving blood sacrifice) the sun would not rise and the world would come to an end. [icon] The Aztec calendar was based on a solar year of 365 days. It consisted of 18 months of 20 days each, [icon] plus 5 extra days. In the center of the famous Aztec calendar stone, the sun god appears. Around it are carvings representing [icon] the Aztec universe. Among the many Aztec artifacts that reflect sun worship are mosaic masks of the sun god made from turquoise and shell inlays ∎

## Procedure

**1.** Glue the sun god pattern on tagboard. Fill in the lines with black marker.

**2.** Cut mosaic pieces from the paper scraps and glue them to the design. Leave the black spaces between the pieces to look like grout. Cut out the sun god.

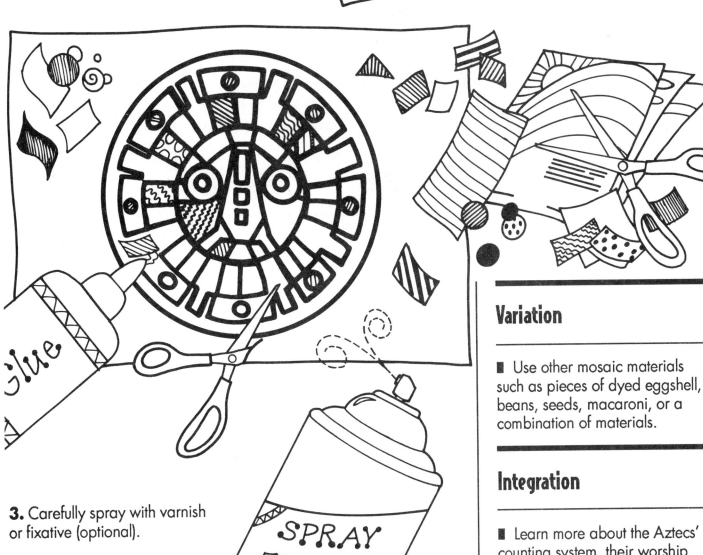

**3.** Carefully spray with varnish or fixative (optional).

## Variation

■ Use other mosaic materials such as pieces of dyed eggshell, beans, seeds, macaroni, or a combination of materials.

## Integration

■ Learn more about the Aztecs' counting system, their worship of the sun, and their remarkable calendar.

See color photo 13.

# Paper Bowl

## Materials

- glue
- brown grocery bags or butcher paper (enough for two 15" circles per student)
- scissors
- leather strips, heavy yarn, shoestrings, or twine for lacing
- hole punch
- markers (optional)
- coarse grained slabs of wood for rubbing
- black or brown crayons with the paper removed

The Indians of the Far North and the Eastern Woodlands made houses, boats, and many different types of utensils and containers out of birch bark. The Indian women who fashioned the utensils and containers needed considerable patience and skill to punch holes in the bark with bone awls, then stitch the seams together with roots, basswood fiber, or animal tendons. Articles of birch bark were often strengthened with pliable tree branches or roots, waterproofed with an application of tree gum, and painted with symbols showing tribal affiliation or ownership ▪

## Procedure

**1.** Simulate birch bark by placing brown paper over a wood surface and rubbing over it with the side of a crayon.

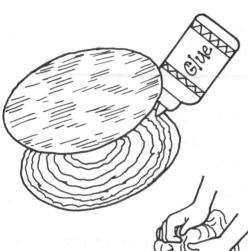

**2.** Cut two 15" circles out of the brown paper. With the crayon sides out, glue the circles together by covering one completely with glue. Crumple, flatten, and allow to dry. This will give you a paper similar to birch bark.

**3.** Cut four small triangles from the outside edge of each circle.

**4.** Punch holes along the edges for binding together.

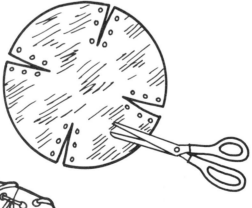

**5.** Bring the sides up and lace them together. (Holes can be punched in the top edge of the bowl and laced for trim.)

## Variation

■ Make an arrow case, or quiver, for carrying arrows to battle. A cylindrical case, it was used for crushable items like feathers.

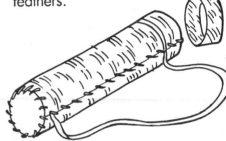

## Integration

■ Make *parfleches*, (rawhide carrying cases used mainly by the Plains Indians) of birch bark paper to carry your school supplies. Lace them together as you did the bowl and decorate them with geometric designs.

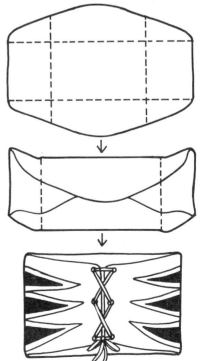

See color photo 30.

# Paper Moccasins

**T**he Indians of the Far North, where the land is often covered with ice and snow, wore moccasins ▢✸▢ out of necessity to protect their feet and allow them to move quickly and quietly through the forest. Some moccasins 〰〰 were waterproofed with tree gum, and some, like the high-top moccasins called *mukluks*, were lined with fur to make them warmer. An Indian's tribe and social rank could be determined by looking ▱◿◺ at his moccasins. Some of the finest examples of Indian beadwork adorn moccasins that belonged to important members of tribe. With a good pair of moccasins, warm leggings, and robes of soft beaver skin, the Indians of the Far North were able to survive the cold northern winters ▪

## Materials

- moccasin pattern on page 106
- scissors
- glue
- brown paper, 12" x 18" (one per student)
- straight pins
- tempera paints, brushes, markers, beads (optional)

## Teacher Preparation

Prepare a moccasin pattern for each student to trace.

## Procedure

**1.** Fold the brown paper, pin the pattern to it, and cut all heavy lines. (This makes two moccasins.)

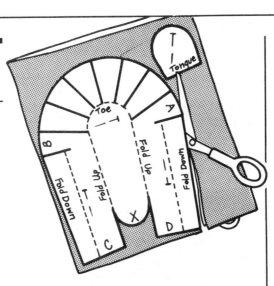

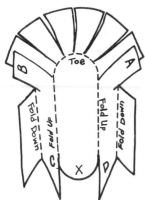

**2.** Fold up the sides and fold down the cuffs on the dotted lines.

**3.** Overlap A and B and glue. Then glue the ends of the other slit sections on top of A/B, alternating from side to side.

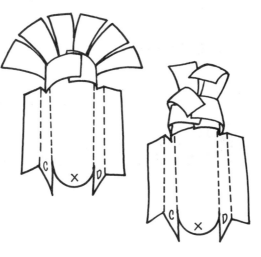

**4.** Cover the glued sections by gluing the tongue over them.

**5.** Overlap sides C and D and glue them to form the heel. Fold up the rounded heel end of the sole and glue it to the sides at the X.

**6.** Decorate with markers and beads (optional).

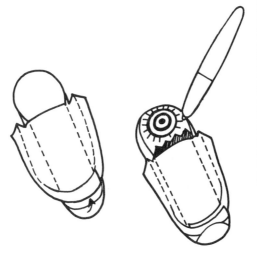

## Variations

■ Make moccasins from fabric or leather to fit your foot.

■ Make tiny moccasins for use as jewelry, or as decorations for packages or invitations.

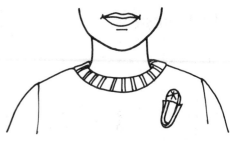

## Integration

■ Put moccasins across a bulletin board. Have students write the name of their favorite storybook character on paper and place it in their moccasin. Then students can share their idea of what it would be like to "walk in the character's moccasins."

See color photo 25.

# Hand Staves

## Materials

- tongue depressors
- assorted markers
- spray lacquer (optional)

**T**he California-Intermountain Indians celebrated the autumn harvest by singing,  dancing, telling stories, and playing games. Everyone, especially the women, spent hours playing or watching the "hand game," a guessing game similar to Button, Button, Who's Got the Button? In another form of the game, one player threw six staves on the ground—three of one design and three of different designs—while the other players guessed which designs would land face up. To make a game stave, a design was made out of bark and fastened to the rounded side of the stick. The stick was then held over the fire until blackened with soot. When the bark was removed, the design remained ∎

## Procedure

**1.** Look at the examples of Native American staves on this page and in other resource books.

**2.** Use the markers to decorate pairs or trios of tongue depressors with similar designs. Do not decorate the back.

**3.** Spray with a coat of fixative if you will be handling the staves.

## Variations

■ Try making staves out of fallen tree limbs you split in half or with tiny branches or toothpicks.

■ Use heavy pieces of tagboard or cardboard to make your staves.

## Integration

■ Play a game of staves and have the class keep score mentally or with tally marks.

■ Have a harvest celebration and play some other Native American games.

■ Research other types of games played by Native Americans.

■ Create another game using the decorated sticks.

SPRAY FIXATIVE

See color photo 12.

# Paper Basket

## Materials

■ strips of newspaper, butcher paper, or brown wrapping paper, 4" x 25" (12 per student)

■ glue

■ stapler

**M**ost American Indian tribes made baskets for storing and transporting their goods. The women of California's Pomo tribe were especially skilled basket makers, weaving long and pliable grasses, plant fibers, and roots of various colors into beautifully patterned baskets. The Pomo also made jeweled gift baskets from downy feathers and shell beads. Some were very large and others were as small as a fingernail ■

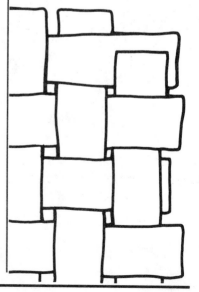

# Procedure

**1.** Fold paper strips in thirds, flatten, and glue the edges.

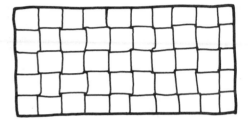

**2.** Lay four strips in vertical lines. Weave four strips across the center of the verticals, reversing each line.

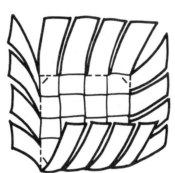

**3.** Staple each corner and fold all strips upward, forming the bottom of the basket.

**4.** Weave four strips through and around the upright strips, making the sides. (Overlap the ends and staple each one to secure.)

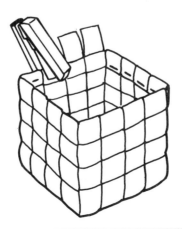

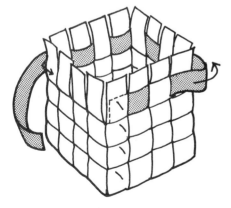

**5.** After the last row, bend and staple the remaining ends of the uprights over the edges.

# Variations

■ Weave various sizes and shapes of baskets with many different types of materials.

■ Weave a small basket from paper drinking straws.

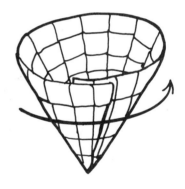

# Integration

■ Make numerical comparisons of the amount of material needed for containers of various sizes.

See color photo 7.

# Owner Sticks

## Materials

- 12" dowels
  (one per student)
- craft sticks
  (one per student)
- plastic container lid
  (one per student)
- scraps of fabric and yarn
- feathers
- beads or colored
  macaroni
- scissors
- glue
- colored construction
  paper scraps
- assorted markers

**T**he nomadic tribes of the Northwest protected and identified their possessions with owner sticks. After a shelter was set up, a cooking fire started, and ▨▨ water drawn, a family's possessions were unpacked and an owner stick was planted in the ground close by. No two owner sticks were alike. Made from saplings about 30" long and decorated with buckskin, porcupine quills, ⋀⋀⋀ feathers, and claws, they displayed symbols denoting the owner's name or position in the tribe. Especially useful during hunts, owner sticks were used to mark each hunter's kill ∎

## Procedures

**1.** Place the craft stick over the dowel, making a cross. Attach the two by wrapping yarn in an "X" fashion.

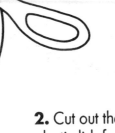

**2.** Cut out the inside of the plastic lid, forming a ring. Wrap the ring with yarn.

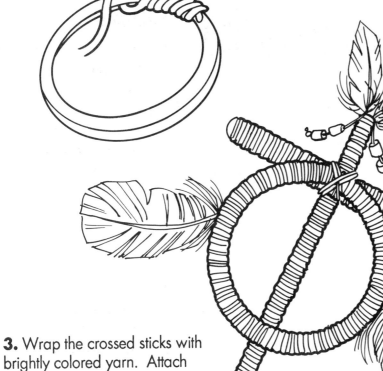

**3.** Wrap the crossed sticks with brightly colored yarn. Attach the ring to the sticks at the intersection. Then personalize the stick by decorating with any of the remaining materials.

## Variations

■ Make small owner sticks with craft sticks or toothpicks.

■ Use drinking straws for sticks and a ring cut from construction paper. Use these small owner sticks to show possession of items in the classroom.

## Integration

■ Make a list of the different ways people in your community identify their possessions.

■ Act out the steps a Native American family of the Northwest Coast would go through to set up camp.

See color photo 40.

# Two-in-One Puppet

## Materials

- paper bags, lunch size (one per student)
- scissors
- assorted colors of construction paper
- glue
- odds and ends
- pencils
- crayons and markers

**T**he Indians of the Northwest Coast were great storytellers. Especially popular were stories in which one character was transformed into another, where a boy became a bird or a coyote turned into a porcupine. At *potlatches* (gift-giving wintertime festivals) and at other festivals, the Indians developed these stories into dramatic performances involving music, dance, costumes, and masks. The most intricate of these carved wooden masks were the transformation masks, which took months to design and make. These masks transformed one character into another; when strings were pulled, the two halves of the mask opened to reveal an inner mask ∎

# Procedure

**1.** Choose two characters for your puppets. They can be human or animal. Using construction paper and other materials suggested, draw, color, cut, and assemble the first character. Glue it onto the front of the paper bag under the flap.

**2.** Draw, color, cut, and assemble the face of a second character. Glue it onto the folded-down flap of the bag. Be sure the second character extends long enough to completely cover the first puppet's face.

**3.** Try operating the puppet and make adjustments if necessary.

## Variations

■ Invent other ways of transforming puppets.

■ Make transformation puppets on the front and back of a paper plate.

## Integration

■ Make another transformation puppet for your other hand, and use the four characters to tell a Northwest Coast legend or story.

■ Make a transformation mask to explain natural phenomenon like day and night, rain and rainbows, or seeds and plants.

See color photo 18.

# Paper-Plate Shield

## Materials

- heavy white paper plate, 9" in diameter (one per student)
- assorted markers
- glue or stapler
- pencil
- feathers (optional)
- tagboard strip or ribbon for shoulder strap, 1½" x 30" (optional)
- tagboard rectangle for bottom panel, 3" x 5" (optional)

## Notes to the Teacher

The following list gives some colors and their symbolic meanings:

**White:** clear water; day

**Black:** growth and the life cycle from birth to death; a black-and-white feather means completeness

**Red:** morning or evening; good health

**Blue:** sky; power and durability

**Yellow:** sunny day; sunny mood

**Orange:** return of calm after a storm; making peace with a friend or enemy

**Gray:** gloom and fatigue

The directions of the compass are also represented by colors: red = north, white = south, yellow = east, and black = west.

**S**hields were used by the Plains Indians when they went into battle. A warrior's shield was his most valuable possession. Made from the thick rawhide of the buffalo's neck or shoulder which had been shrunk to increase it's thickness, the shield protected the warrior from spears, arrows, and even bullets. When not in use, shields were displayed above the warrior's bed or on a tripod in front of his tepee. The designs painted on the shield by the warrior himself were selected to give him special powers. These designs were arranged to represent north, south, east, west, and the earth and sky. Their colors also had symbolic meanings ■

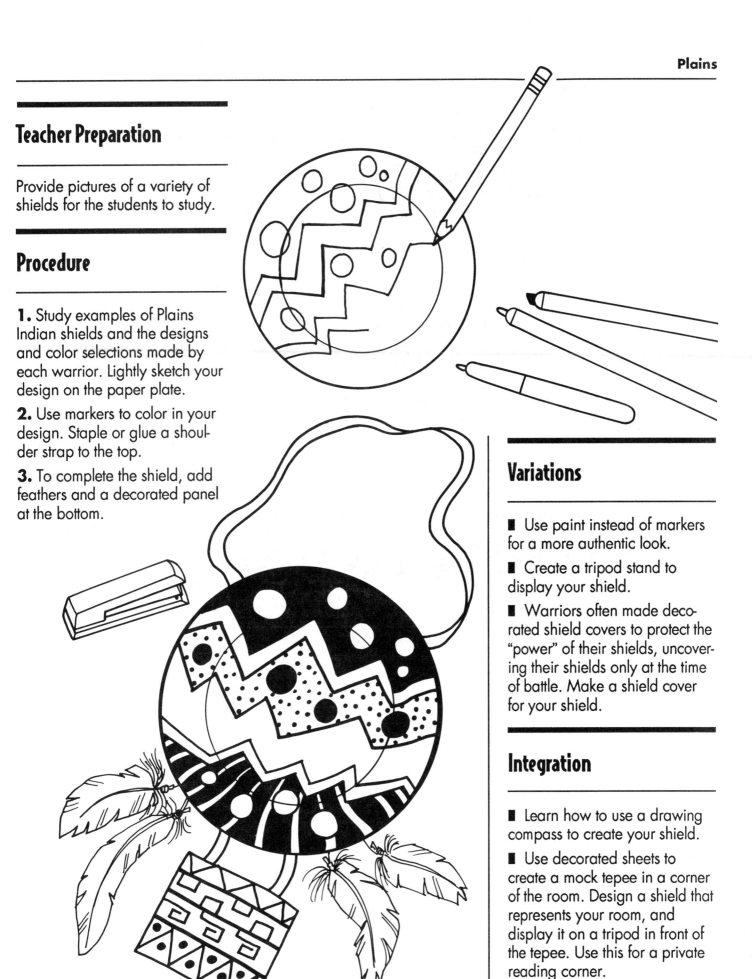

## Teacher Preparation

Provide pictures of a variety of shields for the students to study.

## Procedure

**1.** Study examples of Plains Indian shields and the designs and color selections made by each warrior. Lightly sketch your design on the paper plate.

**2.** Use markers to color in your design. Staple or glue a shoulder strap to the top.

**3.** To complete the shield, add feathers and a decorated panel at the bottom.

## Variations

■ Use paint instead of markers for a more authentic look.

■ Create a tripod stand to display your shield.

■ Warriors often made decorated shield covers to protect the "power" of their shields, uncovering their shields only at the time of battle. Make a shield cover for your shield.

## Integration

■ Learn how to use a drawing compass to create your shield.

■ Use decorated sheets to create a mock tepee in a corner of the room. Design a shield that represents your room, and display it on a tripod in front of the tepee. Use this for a private reading corner.

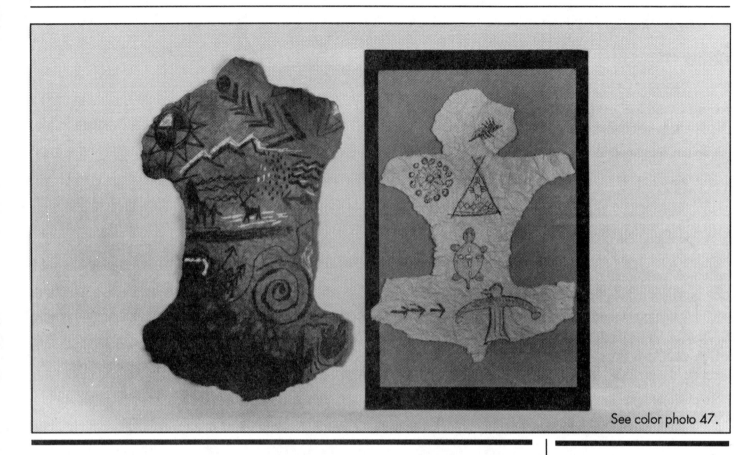

See color photo 47.

# Paper Hide

The Plains Indians,  who depended on the buffalo for food, clothing, and shelter, used buffalo robes as wraps, blankets, bedding, and rugs. Decorated with pictographs, these robes sometimes recorded the passage of the years, the so-called "winter count." Each "winter," or year, was represented by a pictograph of the year's most important event—a war, a solar eclipse, a peace conference, an epidemic, or the like ■

## Materials

■ pictographs from page 108
■ brown butcher paper or a large paper bag (one per student)
■ crayons
■ bucket of water or classroom sink
■ brown tempera paint (1 cup)
■ newspapers

## Teacher Preparation

Reproduce pictographs for each student.

## Procedure

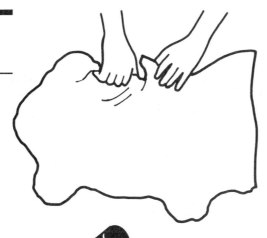

**1.** Tear the shape of a buffalo hide from a large piece of paper. Note: The teacher can provide a pattern if necessary.

**2.** Using the pictographs on page 108 or some of your own, draw pictographs on the "hide," pressing down firmly with the crayons.

**3.** Dilute one cup of brown tempera paint in a bucket or sink full of water.

**4.** Crumple the paper tightly and immerse in the tempera/water solution. Knead the "hide" gently but thoroughly in the mixture. Remove and flatten out to dry on newspapers.

## Variations

■ Prepare a "hide" according to the above directions and make a "winter count" for yourself depicting important events in your life such as your birth, first step, first word, first time on a tricycle, and first day of school.

■ Make several paper hides to use in the construction of a tepee.

■ Make other items out of paper hide.

## Integration

■ Make a list of all the ways the Indians used the buffalo.

■ Make buffalo masks and perform a skit based on a buffalo hunt and the creation of a buffalo robe.

■ Research the significance of the white buffalo robe.

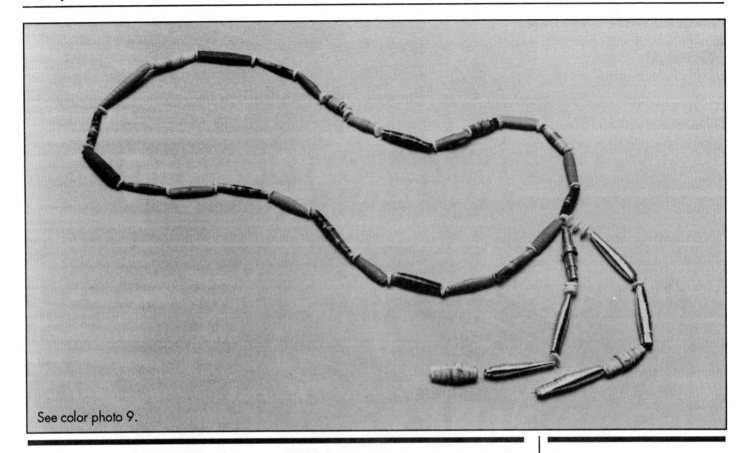

See color photo 9.

# Paper Wampum

## Materials

- wampum bead pattern on page 103
- gift wrap, colorful magazine pages, colorful copy paper, or wallpaper
- scissors
- glue
- toothpicks
- dental floss or elastic thread
- assorted beads (optional)
- white glue
- pencil

The Indians of the Eastern Woodlands used ⚞ wampum as a medium of exchange. Wampum, which consisted of small cylindrical beads made out of clam shells, 𝚼𝚼 was a symbol of wealth and power. Women of the Iroquois tribe made both white and [⫿⫿⫿] purple wampum and wove it into belts, headbands, armbands, and moccasins. Later, white traders ♡ introduced colored glass beads to the Indians, trading them for furs, maize, tobacco, and other commodities ▮

## Teacher Preparation

Prepare the wampum bead pattern for each student to trace.

# Procedure

**1.** Trace the wampum bead pattern on different colored paper and cut it out. To make each bead, place the toothpick at the wide base of the triangle strip. If using decorated paper, be sure it is pattern side down. Bend and roll the paper so it fits tightly around the toothpick.

**2.** Continue to roll the rest of the paper tightly. Put a small dab of glue on the underside of the tip. Hold it down until the glue sets, then carefully remove the toothpick. (Too much glue makes the bead stick to the toothpick.)

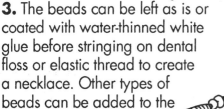

**3.** The beads can be left as is or coated with water-thinned white glue before stringing on dental floss or elastic thread to create a necklace. Other types of beads can be added to the string, if desired.

# Variations

■ Use beads to make bracelets, or sew them onto other items.

■ Use elastic thread and drinking straw beads. Cross lace them to create an expandable bracelet.

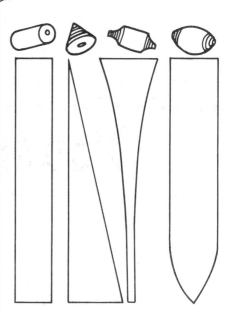

■ Make other bead shapes. Some are included here.

# Integration

■ Use the wampum to "trade" or purchase things from classmates.

■ Read about other forms of "money" used by early people.

■ String the beads into color patterns.

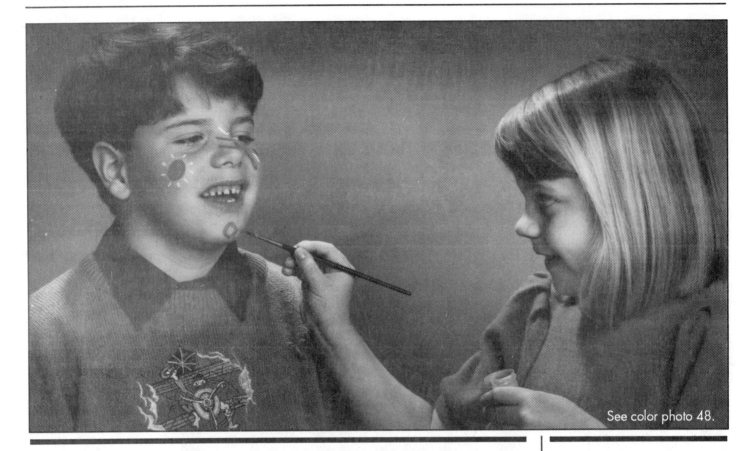

See color photo 48.

# Body Painting

## Materials

- face paints (craft stores or specialty children's stores)
- brushes
- cold cream to remove paints
- soft rags or tissues
- pictographs on page 108
- plain paper (one per student)
- crayons

**T**he Woodlands Indians wore body paint for all important occasions. When the first Europeans saw the New World natives painted a reddish-brown, they began referring to them as "redskins." A mixture of a powdered mineral and animal fat, body paint gave the Indians protection from wind, weather, and insects. The colors and designs of some body painting were symbolic—signifying membership in a special group or recording a brave deed—but most were expressions of personal visions or experiences. Relatives and friends helped apply the body paint over a coating of animal grease, painting designs on the back, eyes, face, and scalp. Some tribes stamped painted patterns on the skin with carved wooden blocks ∎

## Procedure

**1.** Study pictures of Native American symbols and the examples of face painting on this page and in resource books.

**2.** Choose partners and have students make drawings of the symbols they would like to have painted on their faces.

**3.** Students take turns painting one another's faces. Let dry.

**4.** Remove face paintings with cold cream and soft cloths or tissues.

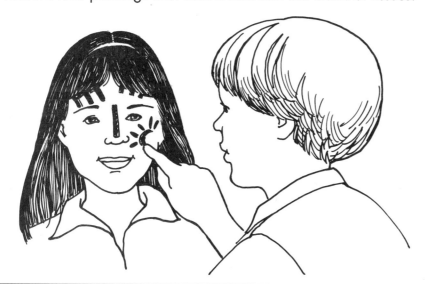

## Variations

■ Cut pictures of celebrities from magazines and paint them with marking pens. Make a collage of these pictures.

■ Draw tattoo designs on your arms with washable markers and wear them for a day.

## Integration

■ Write a short skit about the first meeting between Europeans and the Native Americans.

■ Try making face paint using common food items.

■ Research the purposes for body paint. For instance, is it purely symbolic or does it protect the skin from the sun or bugs?

See color photo 33.

# Rolled Clay Container

- small plastic bowl or margarine tub (one per student)
- waxed paper
- oil, margarine, or nonstick cooking spray
- low-fire clay or air-dry clay
- old soft brush
- damp sponge
- tempera paint and brushes

**T**he Indians of the Southwest have been skilled potters for more than 1,500 years. The Pueblo peoples used clay pots to store, prepare, and serve food; to carry and store water; and to hold ceremonial offerings. All of them used the coil method of making pottery, but each tribe had its own characteristic designs. Because the Indians of the Southwest depended on rain for their survival, cloud symbols appear frequently on their pottery. Geometric shapes, squash blossoms, birds, animals, and kachinas are other popular motifs. Potters from the Santo Domingo Pueblo always left a small gap between the lines painted around a pot. This "spirit path" allowed the spirit that lived in the vessel to leave and return. Without it, the spirit might break the pot in trying to get out ∎

# Procedure

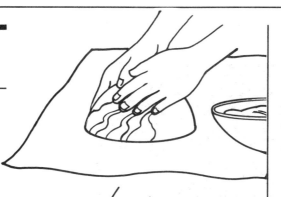

**1.** Working on waxed paper, turn the plastic bowl over and cover with margarine or some other oil.

**2.** Roll several clay snake ropes of the same diameter. (¼")

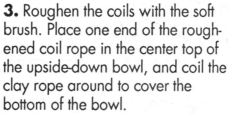

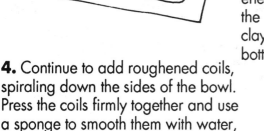

**3.** Roughen the coils with the soft brush. Place one end of the roughened coil rope in the center top of the upside-down bowl, and coil the clay rope around to cover the bottom of the bowl.

**4.** Continue to add roughened coils, spiraling down the sides of the bowl. Press the coils firmly together and use a sponge to smooth them with water, making sure that there are no open spaces.

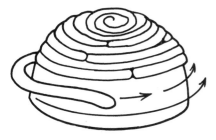

**5.** Dry for several days until hard. Turn the clay bowl right side up and carefully remove the plastic bowl.

**6.** Use the bowl as is, or bake it according to the clay manufacturer's directions.

**7.** Paint Native American designs on the bowl using earth colors.

# Variations

■ Use some of the leftover clay to make beads or medallions.

■ Make small figures and containers with faces on them similar to those made by other groups of Southwest Indians.

■ Make and hide broken pieces of pottery and stage an archaeological dig.

# Integration

■ Read *When Clay Sings* by Byrd Baylor. Paint the pots to resemble the ones in this book.

■ Visit a museum and view Native American pottery.

See color photo 26.

## Materials

- kachina headpiece pattern on page 107
- pictograph pattern on page 108
- white or turquoise light weight cardboard or tagboard, 12" x 18" (one per student)
- strips of tagboard or elastic, 1" x 18", to hold tableta on child's head
- scissors
- stapler
- assorted markers
- tempera paints
- brushes
- feathers (optional)
- pencils

# Kachina Headpiece

The Hopi Indians of the Southwest communicated with their important gods through spirits called *kachinas*. These supernatural beings represented things that were a part of the Indians' daily life, such as rain, clouds, crops, birds, and animals. Many Hopi ceremonies involved kachina impersonators. When these impersonators put on their elaborate masks, they were thought to receive the spirit of the kachina. Represented by dancers and by carved wooden dolls, kachinas wear *tabletas*, headpieces made of two or three wooden panels laced together. The colors and designs on the tabletas are symbolic and serve to identify the kachina, of which there are more than two hundred fifty ∎

## Teacher Preparation

Prepare the kachina headpiece pattern for each student to trace on the tagboard or cardboard. Be sure the bottom opening will fit around the student's face. Reproduce pictograph and symbol patterns for each student.

## Procedure

**1.** Look at examples of kachina headpieces in this book and other resource books. Fold the tagboard in half, trace the pattern of the "steps to heaven" kachina headpiece, and cut it out.

**2.** Use the pictograph and symbol patterns to sketch designs on the headpiece. Color with markers or paint. Add feathers (optional).

**3.** Staple the 1" x 18" strip or elastic to the back of the headpiece close to the head opening, adjusting it to fit around the child's head.

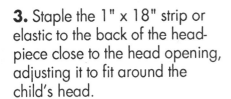

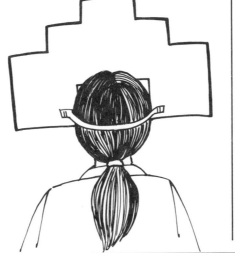

## Variations

■ Design a paper kachina mask and a dance rattle to complete your project.

■ Use a small piece of cardboard and a toilet paper or paper towel roll to create a kachina doll similar to the wooden ones given to children.

## Integration

■ Create your own legends. Write and illustrate them.

■ Learn or invent an Indian dance and perform it for the class. Wear the headpiece.

■ Write a diary page from the point of view of a Hopi child who sees the kachina ceremony for the first time.

*Multicultural Art Activities*

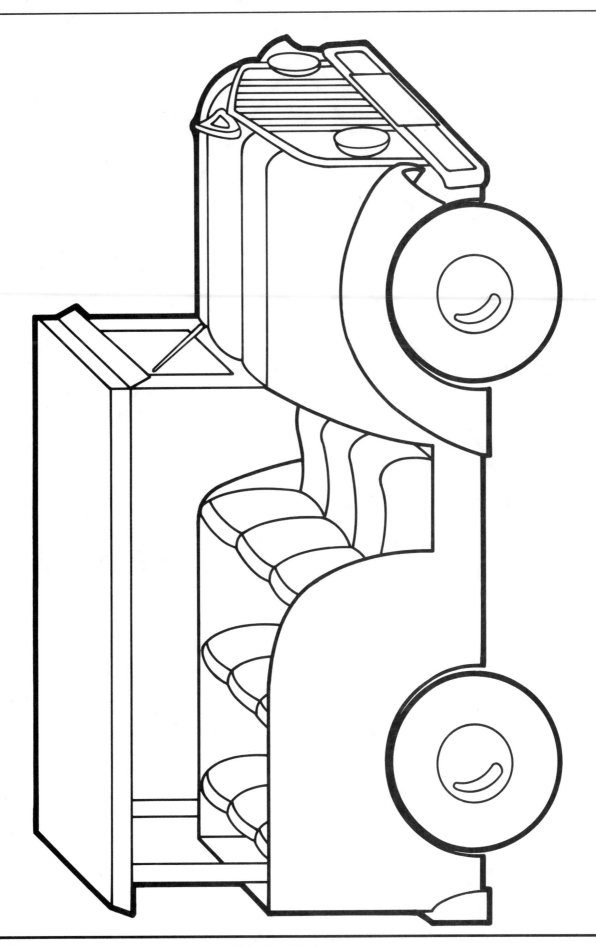

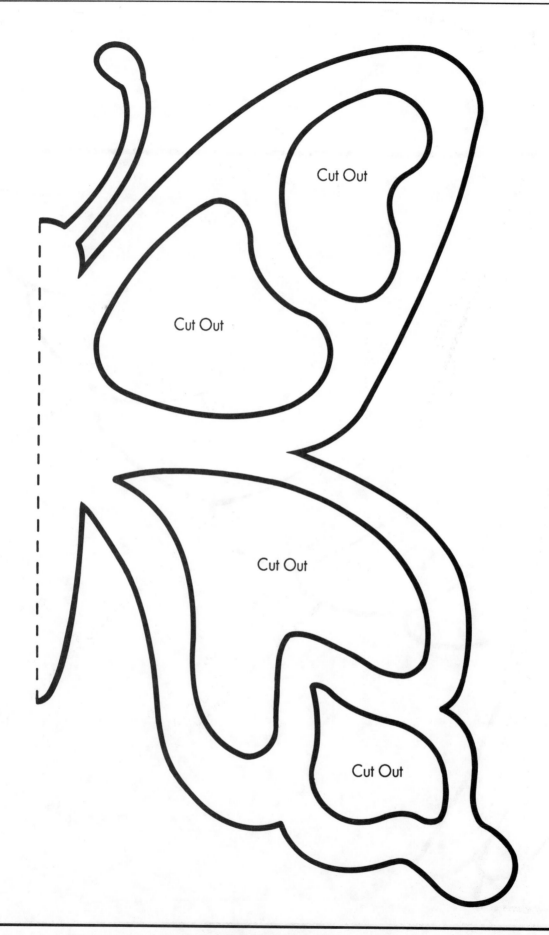

Cut Out

Cut Out

Cut Out

Cut Out

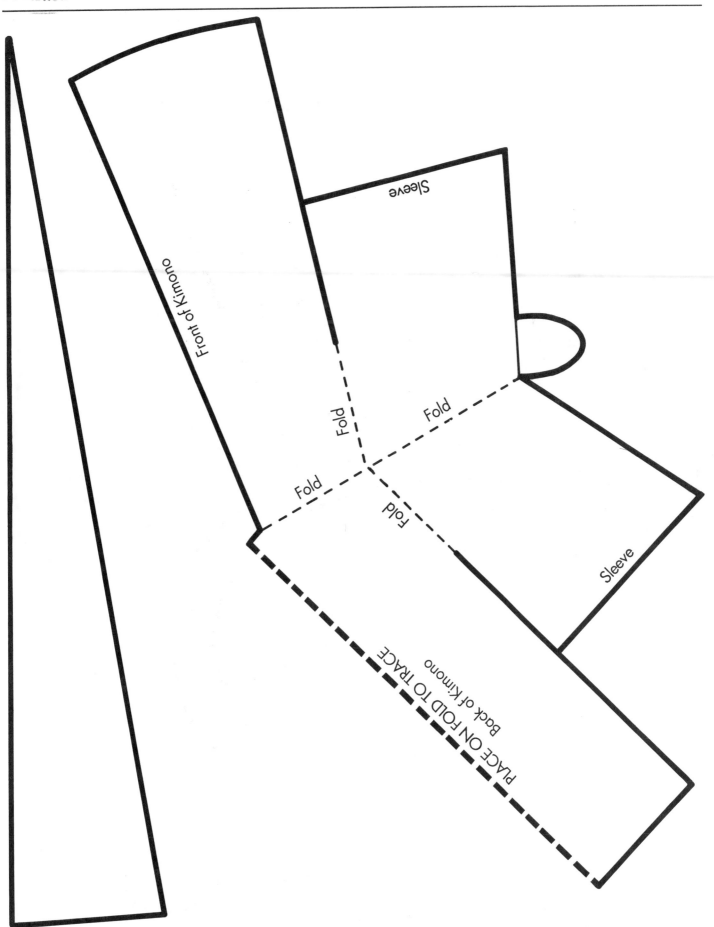

Front of Kimono

Sleeve

Sleeve

Fold

Fold

Fold

Fold

PLACE ON FOLD TO TRACE

Back of kimono

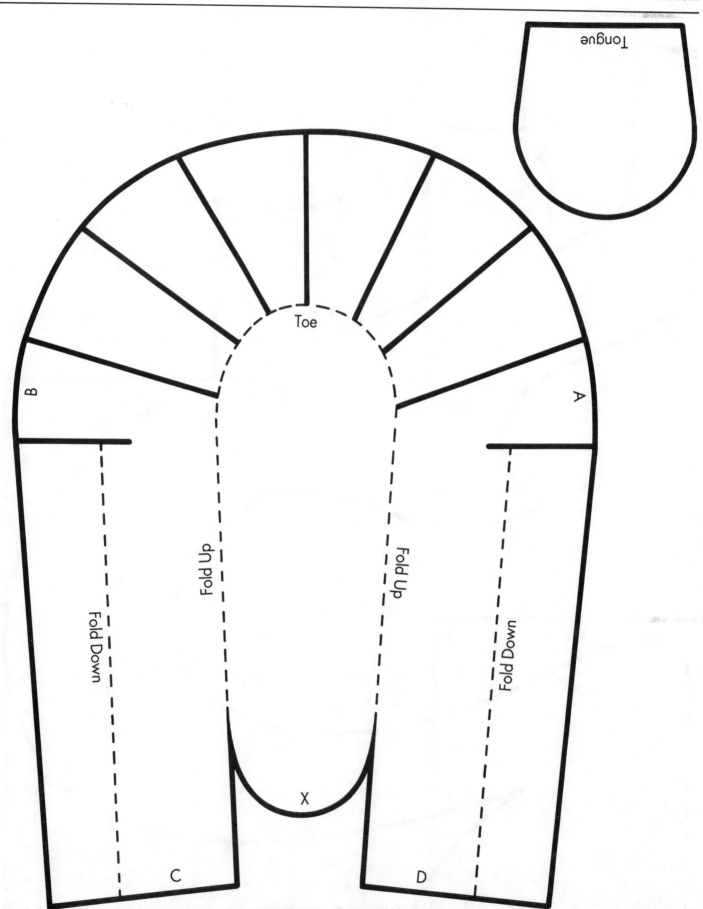

Tongue

Toe

B

A

Fold Up

Fold Up

Fold Down

Fold Down

X

C

D

*Multicultural Art Activities*

Creative Teaching Press

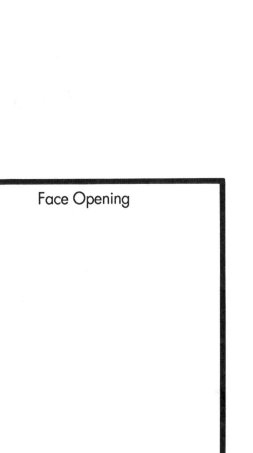

Top

Face Opening

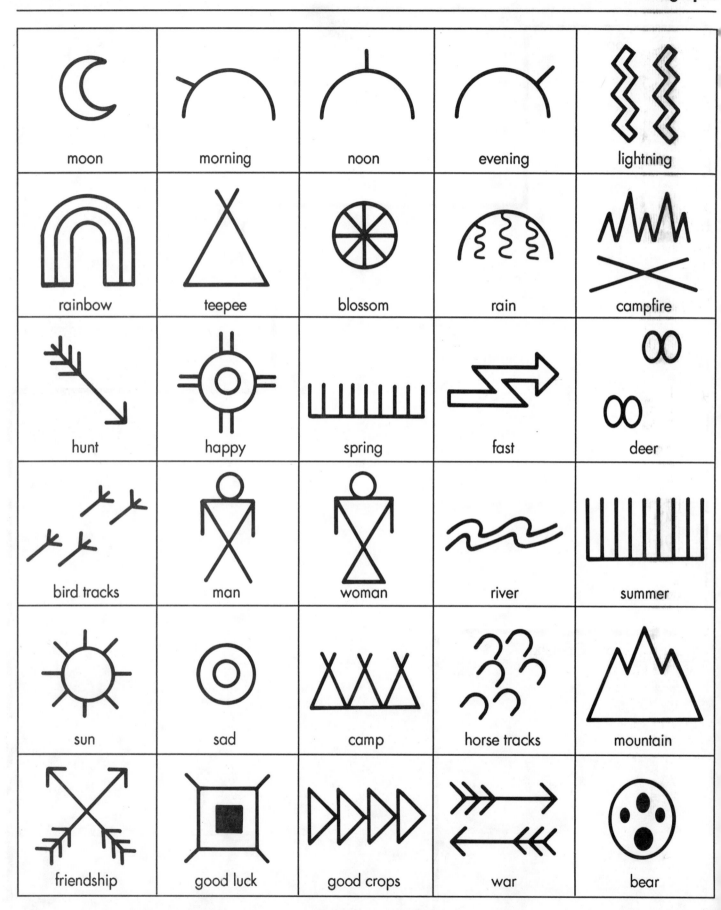

| | | | | |
|---|---|---|---|---|
| moon | morning | noon | evening | lightning |
| rainbow | teepee | blossom | rain | campfire |
| hunt | happy | spring | fast | deer |
| bird tracks | man | woman | river | summer |
| sun | sad | camp | horse tracks | mountain |
| friendship | good luck | good crops | war | bear |